LOOKING BACK
LOOKING BEYOND

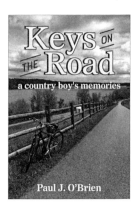

Voices from
Room 6

Keys on
the Road

CT
A Cat's Story

LOOKING BACK LOOKING BEYOND

Paul J. O'Brien

COVER PHOTO | Paul J. O'Brien
BOOK DESIGN | The Troy Book Makers

Printed in the United States of America

The Troy Book Makers • Troy, New York • thetroybookmakers.com

To order additional copies of this title, contact your favorite local bookstore or visit www.shoptbmbooks.com

ISBN: 978-1-61468-579-1

Contents

FOUR FILMS: THEIR ART AND POWER

INDELIBLE MOMENTS FROM THREE FILMS

FICTION

BACK TO THE LIGHT

Dedication

When you look back at the road you have traveled, it's hard sometimes to see how you managed to reach the point you did. When you think about the journey you have taken, you know that there are guides and mentors and moments that were so crucial in shaping you into whom you have become. And in each endeavor or project you have undertaken on your journey, you know that there are people who nudged you and guided you. No book ever gets written without a community of support.

To all those I have traveled with, whether my mentors or students or simply fellow travelers, I say thank you. As the song says, "I get by with a little help from my friends"; we all do. We all need each other. We know the road sometimes gets pretty dark as we have discovered in the late winter of 2020. Yes, we all need each other.

No one has been a closer supporter, mentor, and fellow traveler than my wife Deborah, and I have deep gratitude for the encouragement she always gives me.

I offer a great note of thanks to those who were willing to read the manuscript and offer constructive thoughts: Deborah, my sister Rosemary Nadeau, and my sister-in-law Elizabeth Cole. And then my niece Carolyn Nadeau who took time out of her busy academic schedule at Illinois Wesleyan University to look very carefully at my draft and offer me a myriad of ideas, some which shifted my thinking and allowed me to see my own creation more clearly. A note of thanks to Dan Pepe, former colleague, for his technical and photographic assistance. Finally I thank Meradith Kill from The Troy Book Makers who always brings a positive spirit and a clear guiding hand to the production of a book.

Preface

I had a deadline, and I wasn't sure that I was going to make it. Let me explain. As part of a planning team for the Spring Session of "Books Sandwiched In" at the downtown Schenectady Library, I had offered to review my new book, which I said would be published in plenty of time. The book review date was more than four months away. Time passed. Three copies of my manuscript had been read and edited, all offering helpful suggestions, but the fourth, the one I knew would be most detailed, was still not back. The last editor was my niece, a college professor, who was finishing a busy couple of weeks of teaching before spring break, which, understandably, eclipsed the editing of my book. At that point I spoke with the publisher, who told me that if she got the manuscript at least six weeks before my review deadline, there was a chance I might have the book. I knew it would be a close call. Then almost out of the blue, COVID-19 arrived. Suddenly the issue was resolved. I received an e-mail announcing that all spring events at the library would be cancelled because of the Coronavirus.

Our world has been irrevocably changed by the virus. Patterns of living and ways of relating to each other shifted dramatically. The work force, except the front-liners and those in essential occupations, had to learn to work out of their home, or sadly had to deal with being laid off. My former profession of teaching no longer offered teachers that wonderful second home where they ply their craft and know the warm contact of students — their classroom. Google and Zoom and all kinds of technological relief came in to fill the void. And it wasn't long before each of us knew of someone who had tested positive, and many of us lost someone we knew.

The seismic shift created in our world by the Coronavirus had its immediate effects not only in the spatial behavior each of us put into practice but also in the thinking about the work we do or create and how it plays in this new world. This shift and the salient and insightful comments made by my niece about certain motifs in my text led me to rework some of the text, rewrite the preface, and change the title. I had entitled my new book *To The Legends and Beyond*, but as I kept thinking, I felt that the whole book was really a looking back to a larger picture than evoked by the word legends and that the looking back gave me insight into the movement forward, into the beyond.

Looking Back, Looking Beyond is a collection of non-fiction pieces, poetic and cinematic inspirations, and fiction. There are certain thematic motifs that play both an explicit and implicit role in the book: the idea of guides or mentors we find on our journey, leading us towards a clearer path, but not always; the powerful notion of community — how it binds and holds us together, but also what happens when a community fractures and one has to navigate through the darkness; and finally the idea of art and how art can serve to build community and to guide us into a deeper awareness and appreciation of life.

Dodging Florence

When we speak of legends, we speak of stories that are popular, old, and to a degree historical but colored by time and imagination. When we speak of a legendary person, we imagine a person or character of some accomplishment or fame; for example, Robin Hood or King Arthur. When we talk about the Legends at Myrtle Beach, South Carolina, we are talking about five award-winning golf courses that draw golfers from all over the East Coast. And that's where this book begins — at the Legends Golf Course in Myrtle Beach in the fall of 2018 when eight golfers arrived to play golf, thinking that they could outlast another visitor who had also decided to visit Myrtle Beach — Hurricane Florence.

Just after we, well four of us, had showed our boarding passes and started down the ramp to the plane, the airline employee checking tickets turned to us and said, "Gentlemen, you do know there will be no return flight from Myrtle Beach. Your call." I remember quickly looking at the other three with me and then back at Larry, the one who had organized the whole trip, but had not yet reached the boarding pass checkpoint. I think the four of us took a step back as if collectively signaling, "That's it, we ain't going," just as Larry, after looking at the two with him, Kevin, his brother, and Jeff, an old friend, lifted his right arm high and then dropped it to shoulder level and pointed down the

1

ramp. "Too much planning with this baby; we're going," he said and handed his boarding pass to the airline checker.

And so it was on. Four days at the Legends Golf Resort in Myrtle Beach, South Carolina, with three days of golf on outstanding courses, but the Thursday return date was now an issue. Larry had been at the Legends a number of times, loved the golf packages they offered, and the restaurants and bars that provided evening fun. No question that Larry had worked hard at promoting the trip and doing a lot of logistical work organizing all the details, including such things as notifying us that Dick's had a great sale on golf club travel bags. And everything had come together smoothly: plane tickets and seating, room accommodations at the Legends, reservations for dinners, course information. Larry, above all, was ready. He had been fine-tuning his game, and he was eager to take on the best of the Legends.

Running counter to Larry was Hurricane Florence, coming up the Coast and looking for some land to create havoc on. The forecast indicated that Flo wouldn't hit until late Thursday, leading Kevin to say, "Hey, we get in our three days of golf and get going Wednesday afternoon — should be fine." Larry and Jeff nodded in agreement, though the four of us who were ahead on the ramp looked at each other with eyes of trepidation.

It was smooth sailing on Elite Airways, and we landed on schedule in the middle of a sultry Sunday afternoon. I had never experienced UBER before, but Kevin was cool as a shore breeze as he navigated the UBER experience for us. I had the advantage of riding shotgun in our car, and listening to our driver Jimmy, a long-haired, rail-thin dude who played drums in a band when he wasn't driving. "Hey," he said, "got a good one for ya." The four of us perked up. "Guy gets up to heaven and starts to settle in when he hears some pretty good drumming. He turns to St. Pete and says, 'Sounds like Buddy Rich.' And Pete turns to him and says, 'Nah, just God pretending to be Buddy Rich.'" He laughed, and we joined him. "Listen, guys, I love it down here. Myrtle Beach is where it's at. Don't let this hurricane throw you off. Just settle in, get loose, and enjoy." His advice was refreshing — like an ice cube added to a warm drink.

The Condos were excellent: two units right across the Street from each other. Each unit had two bedrooms with twin beds, two full baths, a large kitchen, and a relaxing living room. In one unit were the four people who had momentarily frozen in the airport at the announcement that there would be no return flight — at least two of us had — Cousin Norm and me, the other two had appeared somewhat concerned: cousin Bill and Dave, a former co-worker of Larry's. In the other unit, the fearless foursome: Larry, our commander, his brother Kevin, friend Jeff, and former neighbor Tommy, a slightly shorter version of Tim Tebow, now working in medical marijuana investments in Florida.

After we had unloaded our stuff, our foursome headed over to Larry's condo for beers and snacks provided by Tommy. As we began to climb the stairs to their second floor living quarters, Norm, who was right behind me, grabbed my arm and said, "You know, this weather thing is pretty scary. I just heard they may close the airport on Tuesday at noon." I mumbled something like "Oh, crap." Just before we reached the top of the stairs, Norm said, "This is serious, we better start making plans about getting out of here."

After a couple rounds of beers and some chips and dip, we headed back to our unit to clean up a bit for dinner, tonight at the Ailsa Pub and Sports Bar at the Legends. One of the claims of the place was that it was a "Scottish-style golf course pub," and that would be nice change of pace. I had just settled in for a minute to check out the TV when my phone lit up — it was Debbie.

"Hey there," I said, "What's going on?"

"You have to think about getting out of there. I was just talking to Linda in Charleston, and she says that they expect to get hit pretty hard."

"I know, we are keeping an eye on things. Not supposed to come on shore until late Thursday."

"Well, that may be, but you may be underestimating this storm. I know you told me that there was no return flight out of Myrtle Beach, but we can pay for you to get a flight out of the nearest open airport."

"Damn," I said, "I don't even know what that would be — and how to get there, unless maybe a bunch of us rented a van or pooled our money for some type of hotel bus."

"Listen," she was pretty serious, "I don't want you trapped down there in a hurricane. The nearest could be Wilmington, North Carolina."

"Ok, listen, we are about to head out for some dinner, so I will try to get a sense of what people are thinking."

"Paul, you don't have to be a daredevil or something — I'd rather have you home safe and sound."

"I know, ok, we will talk in a while. Don't worry too much now."

· · · · ·

The Ailsa Pub was not crowded, and so it was easy to put together a table for 8. As far as the Scottish influence, I didn't see much that was different from your standard sports' bar — the main note a plethora of wide-screen televisions tuned into football. I did notice fish and chips on the menu. With the beers at the Condo and the beers flowing now, our spirits were getting revved up. The football games rumbled across the many screens, with an occasional Hurricane warning, which caused Norm to come to full alert and fixate.

"We're opening on the Moorland Course tomorrow," Larry announced. "Bill, Norm, Dave, and Paul in the first group — you'll tee off at 9:36. Our group will be right behind you. Lunch at the turn. Make sure you are loaded up with water."

"What's the ruling on the pot bunkers again?" Jeff asked.

"Two swings and then you throw it out," Larry took a big swig of his beer. "We're not spending half our day in those. And remember, your maximum score is twice the par."

"I'll drink to that," said Tom, lifting his glass high in the air.

· · · · ·

Back at the Condo, Norm and I sat with a beer watching the weather report and the coming of Florence. Things looked ominous. "You know what," Norm said, sitting up, "I'm checking tonight to see what other airports are still open. I really think we should get the hell out of here."

Norm and Debbie were on the same wave length. "Well, I agree it looks bad, but maybe we should try to get one round in before we make a move." Norm looked at me with kind of a benign scowl and then said, "We'll see. I have to hit the sack. Tired out."

· · · · ·

The large dining facility, a major wing of the clubhouse, offered breakfast buffet style and was buzzing with golfers.

For the moment the weather had taken a back burner, and good food — buffet style — plus the anticipation of the challenging course dominated the thinking. Larry was pumped, "Listen, guys," as he directed a piece of sausage toward his knife, "the Moorland course is no joke. Anyone breaking a 100 here — not too shabby — really." Jeff took a slug of his coffee and then said, "Hey, listen, if I manage to still be standing in this heat after 18, that'll do it for me, but I am revved up." Tommy, sitting at the end of the table, had a tall silver travel mug right in front of him, "Listen up, guys, you just have to know how to do it right!" He took a long drink from his mug and then laughed, "Come onnnn, just got to do it right, men!"

We were led out to the first tee by a congenial guy who seemed to be some type of course manager. He gave us a few tips on how to play the first hole, a 345 yard, par 4. And then with a "Play Well, Gentlemen," he was gone. I remember hitting second after Cousin Bill opened with a nice shot down the center. All I could see was a long sand trap on the right as I came around with my swing, and thank God, the ball went left but not too far left. Dave and Norm had decent shots, and we were off. I was impressed with Dave, especially after Larry had told me about the numerous operations he had gone through on his knees and back. The closest anyone came to a par on hole one, however, was a double bogie, and that set the stage for the day. Larry was right — the course was no joke.

The heat kept us under siege as we navigated the course, every so often one of us disappearing in a pot bunker that was placed strategically. We could see our other foursome laboring behind us, but more often we could hear their shouts, an occasional profanity slipping through the heavy air. Pars were at a premium: no question, the course was winning.

At the turn we staggered into a small dining facility located in the rear of the clubhouse — sandwiches, chips, cold sodas, and water. No one was eager to step back out, but Larry, our captain, tried to fire us up, "Better head out, we don't want to miss our turn." Tommy, with a smile, lifted his mug in the air, "We gotcha, Boss."

Norm spotted the clouds. "They don't look too good—wonder if we will make it through the back nine." Larry looked up quickly and then said, "We should be fine. We'll get it done." And Tommy added, "We'll kick some serious ass."

By the 13th hole the rain was coming down, and by the time we reached the 323 yard 14th, the rain was heavy. Approaching my second shot on the fairway, I looked at the green, which was now a pond. I shouted to Bill, "How do we putt in two inches of water?" He threw down his cig, and said, "Damn it, we're out of here." His words were gold. I jumped on the cart, and we headed to the clubhouse. This golf day was over.

Back in the Clubhouse with a hundred or so other soaked golfers, we ordered a brew and a few of us became fixated on the weather commentary running along the bottom of taped programs about farthest drive contests or how to blast out of the sand. "Geez," Norm said, looking at the reports of Florence nearing the mainland, "this is a monster."

· · · · ·

"Hey, Guys, listen up." Larry had approached us, not looking quite as drenched as the rest of us — because of his new rain jacket purchased at Dick's. "We got Rioz tonight — Steak like you won't believe. Brazilian stuff. You will love this place, so, in a few we'll get the van back to the Condos, shower, relax for a while, and then we'll UBER to the restaurant. Let's say in my Condo at 6. I'm telling you, bring your appetite to this place because you are going to eat, and then Crocodile Rock — oh man, wait till you see these guys. Great night ahead!"

Back at the Condo, Norm started pacing as he watched the ominous reports on the television. "Listen, I am ready to make a move. We got to get out of here. They are starting to shut down everything." I had just looked at my texts from Debbie whose basic message was "You need to make a move — or else you are going to be stuck there."

"What's your thought, Norm?"

"I am calling for a rental. Are you in?"

"Probably yes," I said, still not totally committed to leaving.

"I talked to Bill and Dave. They're not sure, but they might want to get out if the report gets any worse." As Norm started dialing, I stepped into the bedroom to head for the shower. When I returned to the television room, Norm looked exasperated. "I got it almost set and then I had problems with my phone — not sure what's wrong. Here's the number. Can you call and complete the deal?"

I hesitated for a second and then said, "Sure."

All set. We could pick up the SUV, anytime after 7. I would deal with the credit card issue when we got to the rental. "Let's go tell them what's going on," Norm said, and all four of us headed out to make our case to Larry and the other three. On the way out the door, a woman pulled up in a car marked "Legends" and handed us a piece of paper. "Info about tomorrow," she said.

· · · · ·

The Memorandum, from Joe Flore Jr. (FDM), was directed to "All Guests" of the Legends. The text pointed out that the Legends was "staying current" on Hurricane Florence, and although it was not directly in the hurricane's pathway, there were concerns. As long as the resort had power, they would assist us in whatever way they could. "Route 501, the main highway, would be one way starting at 12 noon 9/11/18 and would remain that way until further notice. No traffic can travel from Legends east after 1200hrs tomorrow. Please be aware we will not have any housekeeping service available for you and as such we are dropping off extra towels and wash cloths on 9/11/18. Services will be at a minimum."

· · · · ·

Kevin was heated. "Look, there is no reason to leave tonight. We are fine. The freaking hurricane isn't supposed to hit until Thursday night." Tommy jumped in, "Look, what's a little hurricane — we can handle this. We are good to go." Jeff raised his bottle of beer — "I'm with you guys."

Norm interrupted, "We are dead by noon tomorrow. There is no traffic into Myrtle Beach where the rentals are. And the traffic going in before that will be crazy. We can roll tonight and get started before it all goes crazy."

"I am telling you we are ok," Kevin countered. "Listen, first thing in the morning, I will drive into Myrtle Beach and rent a van big enough for seven. I get back here, we get in our eighteen holes, and we head out tomorrow afternoon. No problems."

"And by the way, guys," Larry said, "I talked to the people here at Legends and we will get a refund for the day we don't play, but if it were up to me I would stay and play me some golf."

"Kevin, what about going tonight and getting that van," Norm said. "Then we can pack and be ready to go first thing in the morning if we have to."

"I will go first thing in the morning, and that's it! We will be fine!" Kevin took a long drink of his beer. "We can be all packed and ready, come back right after 18, and then get the hell out of here."

I looked at Norm and nodded. I had to make one more move before dinner — call the rental car agency and cancel our booking. We were moving closer to the edge — Florence was coming in — but this evening would be our counter punch.

· · · · ·

The meat was flying through the air to the beat of spirited Brazilian music: beef, pork, chicken, and lamb wielded on long wooden skewers by dashing waiters. "I told you this place was awesome," Larry shouted at our table located in the middle of the floor at Rioz Brazilian Steakhouse. I am not a big meat guy, but the restaurant had a huge salad bar, and I had filled my plate with a rich array of veggies and cheeses. A slab of medium rare beef landed on Larry's plate, and he fired a thumb's up at the waiter. Then he lifted his glass: "Here's to a great round of golf tomorrow." We lifted our glasses of wine and beer, then drank, and the night played on. Florence for the moment had receded from everyone's mind.

Following the rich and delicious dinner, Larry led us outside and down the street, through a park, and across a few more crowded streets until we arrived at Crocodile Rock, a large bar and club where the central focus was a stage with two pianos. It wasn't packed but there was a good crowd. "Get a beer and let's grab those seats along the left side," said Tommy, "good view from there."

We settled in along the rail, Bill to my right and Norm to my left. The music was cranking up, and we got into it too, encouraged by the two guys playing the pianos. "Run-around Sue" was rolling, and the crowd was hopped up, singing along. I leaned over to Bill and said, "Good stuff." He laughed and said, "Can't beat it."

Behind and to the left of the piano player on our side — the two players faced each other — was a sign that said "Three Words or Less," with a blackboard underneath it. For a few bucks you could have words of your choice written on the black board; you could also write down the name of a song on a piece of paper, put some money with it, and place both on the piano near you. The phrases that popped up — "Go Red Sox" to "Beat the Yankees" to — and one of OUR guys slipped this one in — "Fuck the Yankees."

The beer was flowing, the music rocking. Larry walked up with a slip of paper, dropped some money in the jar, and the piano player, who was just finishing a song, glanced at it, and immediately launched into "Pour Some Sugar on Me."

All of us seemed to have forgotten about the coming storm, even when the words "Fuck Florence" were written on the board, causing a big roar from the crowd. We were done with a couple rounds of drinks when the request for "American Pie" came in, and that brought the crowd together, singing as loudly as they could, "And them good old boys were drinking whiskey and rye / Singin' this'll be the day that I die / This'll be the die that I die."

· · · · ·

The following morning, Kevin and Tommy set out for Myrtle Beach Airport to rent a van while the rest of us packed and then gathered in the almost empty clubhouse restaurant. "There's some food out, guys," the waitress said, "and you'll have to do the best you can with everything. We are really short-handed today."

"Any word from Kevin," Norm asked as Larry walked up to the table.

"Just talked with him. He's in line to rent a van, a few people ahead of him. Should be ok."

"That's good," Bill said. "What's our tee time today?"

"I think it's 9:05 — Parkland Course, and Kev and Tommy should be with us. Same grouping as yesterday, except Dave is with our group and Kevin is with Bill's group."

. . . . .

Just as we were about to load the golf carts, Tommy walked up. 'All good," he said. "Kevin is parking the van. Not a problem." He took a swig from his silver mug.

I could see Kevin walking across the lawn toward us, and as I gazed back at the course, I was struck by the contrast with yesterday, when golfers were lined up to start the day. Today not a soul, and we had the only four carts in sight. "You guys pretty much have the course to yourselves today, fellas," the starter said. "Stay dry."

Kevin was talking to Larry, and I could see that both were animated, a mixture of concern and sudden bursts of laughter. Then I heard Larry say, "Jesus!" And Kevin shook his head and laughed. He was riding with me, and I had loaded his clubs on the driver's side since he knew this course.

The heat was pressing in again as we teed off, but this morning the sun was buried behind clouds. "How'd it go in town with the rental?" I asked Kevin as we started down the first fairway.

"Jesus, you won't believe it, but we got really lucky, really lucky."

"Got the last van?" I asked.

"God," Kevin said as he grabbed his water mug, "this weather is a bitch and even without the sun. Ok, got to tell ya what the hell happened. I'm feeling like a bit of a shit, but listen, I got us a van."

"What'd ya do, throw an old couple out of a van and steal it?"

"Let's hit this shot, and then I'll give you the story. Tommy knows and so does Larry."

Kevin stopped the cart about ten feet from my ball, and I took out my number two fairway wood and took a hard swing, catching it a little behind and sending it up in the air about eighty yards down the course. I jumped back in and Kevin drove ahead to his ball. He hit a strong five iron which headed straight at the green and then turned towards the sand trap on the right — "Shit," he yelled. "I'm in."

I looked to my right and both Bill and Norm seemed to be struggling in a rough patch of high grass. Bill swung and the ball popped ahead about thirty feet. Norm was still looking for his ball.

Back in the cart, Kevin took another slug of water and then began, "So Tommy drops me off at the rental center about 7:30. He is going to circle the airport until he is sure I have a van. The fucking place is packed. Budget especially. So I'm in line for 15 minutes and it's not moving at all. At one point I look up and see Budget Fastbreakers. If you are a member, you can jump in another line. Fastbreakers had zero people in the line!" He slowed the cart down near my ball. "Go ahead."

I jumped out, took my eight iron and made a solid connection driving the ball right over the green and off the other side. "Shit," I say and jump back on.

"So, I look up on my phone on how to join. Very simple. Name, e-mail address, credit card, license number. So I joined. And in a minute they send me a confirmation email. So, I'm all set but I feel guilty — I had been standing in line with these people, which now extended ten behind me. Could I actually do it?" He laughed. "Just then Tom called as he circled. I whispered what I was thinking of doing. As if he was either a Devil or an Angel on my shoulder. He said, 'Do it. You will never see these people again. Plus any one of them could have done the same thing. You were just smarter.' With that little push, I stepped to my left and walked right to the front. I could hear the people wondering what I was doing." Norm and Bill were both on the green now. "The counter woman called next. 'Someone step forward.' "I said, 'Excuse me. I'm a member of your Fastbreaker.' My heart was racing. My membership was actually active for less than ten minutes. It worked!

"Less than ten minutes later, I was walking to our van. If I had stayed, I would have been in line another hour, and it didn't look as if there were that many keys on the wall where the first line was heading. Fifteen minutes, I was back here. Goal accomplished."

"God," I said, "we could have been up shit's creek. No planes and no van." We pulled up to the right of the sand trap. Kevin's ball was buried pretty well in front of a steep bank.

"Look at the damn ball," he said, reaching for his sand wedge.

"Heh, Kev, you got the van — that's what counts," and I raised my right hand for a high five.

· · · · ·

The heat and humidity grew more oppressive, and the skies turned more menacing as we forged ahead. Norm was slowing way down and indicated he was getting ready to throw in the towel. Bill, the old vet, stoically fought on. Kevin regaled me with stories about his company's trip to Vegas. None of us was breaking the course record, but there was light. I could hear euphoric shouts from our trailing foursome. And I had noticed Tommy high-fiving Larry on the green of the second hole and Larry holding his putter high in the air on the fourth hole.

On the seventh hole, Norm sat in the cart — "I'm done," he said. "The heat is killing me." Bill, Kevin, and I teed off into what we could see in the distance was rain starting to fall. "Crap, here we go again," said Bill. By the time we reached our fairway shots, the rain had reached us, not too hard yet, and so we played on. By the ninth hole, we knew our fate was sealed. Putting out on the lake-like ninth, we heard another euphoric shout and "Yes" from our trailing foursome. I looked back and saw Larry lift his ball from the cup on the eighth. We were done, and we headed for the clubhouse in the strong rain.

In the cavernous building, we had just ordered a sandwich from an improvised menu when Larry and his crew walked in. He looked pretty dry, the jacket was key, and he had a big smile. "You look pretty happy," Kevin said. "Oh, Man!" Larry said, as Tommy handed him a beer, "My putter was so hot — 6 one putts. And I shot 44 for the 9." Jeff stepped forward, "I say we do another 9. What's a little rain?" Norm almost gagged on his sandwich, and Jeff burst out laughing, "Only kidding — it was getting a little too wet out there — still if we wait a while." Norm was staring at him, "Look, Kevin got the van for us — we have to get the hell out of Dodge as soon as possible."

"Norm's right," said Kevin. "Finish a quick lunch, head back to our condos, grab a shower, put some dry clothes on, load the van, and head north."

"Guys," Larry said, "I'll see the manager about the discount he promised us before we leave."

· · · · ·

We were loaded and ready: seven golf travel bags standing in the back of the van, Jeff in seat four with suitcases, Norm and Bill in seat three, Larry and Dave in seat two, and Kevin driving with me in shotgun. We were heading north out of the reach of Florence; Tommy in his red Dodge Ram was heading back to Florida.

Route 501 was not as crowded as I had thought it would be, but after a mile, we turned right, and we were now in the hands of Kevin at the wheel with his Google Map showing him the way. Within minutes we were out of the suburbs and into the country. Looking out, it seemed to me that we had driven into an episode of "Twilight Zone," on a country road with only an occasional car in sight. I half expected to see a farmer, his disabled tractor off in a field, try to flag us down and point to some alien he had run over. Kevin, who is a natural story teller, kept the tales rolling — more adventures in Vegas, a trip to Notre Dame University with Larry and his Pop, memories of funny and sad things at St. Clare's Hospital — and then we saw a sign for Route 95 North.

"Pretty cool route. You wouldn't even know there was an evacuation," I said to Kevin.

"I just followed Google Maps," he said. "Nothing more than that."

And, yes, to my amazement, we were on the ramp for "Route 95 North."

· · · · ·

With the rain coming down harder and the traffic much heavier, we started heading up 95. We knew we had a long ride ahead — 13 or so hours from home. Suddenly a burst of laughter shot over my left shoulder. I turned and Larry was holding his cell phone in a horizontal position. Lewis Black was on — talking about weather forecasters, " I don't know what's worse — the weather or the weathermen. Ok. A couple of years ago in New York City we had a blizzard, and our weatherman at the time was Al Roker, you know Al. Ok, he predicted before the blizzard — which is an emergency condition by the way — he predicted we would have 4 to 12 inches of snow. We had 36 inches of snow! Now giving him the benefit of the doubt, he's two feet off. That's not even close. If you were a roofer, and you built a roof and it was two feet off, you'd still be in prison." Dave was roaring and said, "This guy is hilarious." And for the next hour, we had Black — on weather forecasters, politicians, and actors.

At one point, Larry put Black on hold and said, "We got to get a little bite to eat. Let me Google the restaurants in the area." Within seconds, "Got one — Ralph's Barbecue in Weldon — about ten miles farther. One of the reviews says, 'Best Chicken, Brunswick Stew, and BBQ I ever had.' This sounds good, nothing beats good BBQ. And you know down here, they know what they're doing. Here it says, 'North Carolina's Best BBQ.' I'm in!"

"Larry, you're the man," Jeff called from the back.

I am not sure who saw it first — Larry, Kevin, or Norm. Underneath the name "Ralph's" located at the dead center of the building, there were five promotional pigs spaced out over the awning. "Larry," Kevin said, "only one pig is lit up out of five. Is that a bad sign?"

"We'll see in a minute," Larry said, bursting into laughter as he hopped out of the van.

At the door, we were greeted by a woman at a desk with, "Are you guys doing take-out or eating here?" Larry spoke up, "We're here."

"Well," she said, "grab a plate and go to town."

We entered the cafeteria-like restaurant, the buffet to our left. I remember thinking that it was one of the weaker-looking buffets I had seen, kind of dimly lit, but there was a big tray of ribs and a stack of fried chicken. Potatoes, beets, mixed salad, corn, grits, bread, some mixed fruit, a peach cobbler, next to which stood a tall can of whipped cream — not much else. We loaded up with what was there and took our plates to a table nearby. "Well, at least it's food," Norm said as he sat down.

"You ought to see this place when all the pigs are lit," Kevin said, and burst out laughing.

I do remember everyone ate with gusto, a few went back for seconds, and then the peach cobbler loaded with whipped cream wrapped it up. Back on the road, Norm was at the wheel, and Kevin had dropped back into his seat.

I had thought about volunteering a shift at driving, but as I looked at the highway through the front windshield, I felt as if I was looking through a glazed window, and with the rain added to that, I knew I would have a hard time. We were now into Virginia with heavy traffic and rain, and I thought it was my duty to keep Norm awake by talking. We spent some time chatting about creatures in the attic, and the danger of electrical fires — Norm is an electrician — and then we shared stories about Galway Lake where Norm has a camp, and Raquette Lake where my wife's family has a house.

And then Larry fired up some more Lewis Black, and we were laughing again, as we drove onward into the night. Randal Patrick McMurphy leading the inmates home from the fishing expedition.

Once Norm tired after entering New Jersey, we stopped for a coffee and a bathroom. I stood outside the van as Jeff stepped out, a bit stiff from being scrunched in the back. "How ya holding up back there?" I asked him

"Not bad," he said, "I actually don't mind being stuffed in the back. I will be happy though to get home still in one piece."

"You were in it all the way," I said.

"Oh yeah, the minute we got to our rooms. Some people were like let's get outta Dodge without touching a club, and others were like let's just try to get some golf in. It's what we came here for. No way did I want Florence to totally ruin this trip. Probably good we kicked out when we did though — it might have gotten rough."

"Ok, Guys, let's roll," Larry said as he climbed into the driver's seat. Kevin moved to the shotgun position, and Norm and I took over the second seat. It was well after mid-night, the rain was more of a drizzle, and most of us, except Larry and Kevin, were drifting into sleep. As I recall, Larry got us into New York. One more stop, and then back with Kevin for the final stretch. It seemed right that Kevin who had commandeered this van through a daring and deft move have the final lap back into Rotterdam.

It was about 6:00 a.m. when we touched down, and started to drop members off — Bill, Dave, Jeff, and Norm. Kevin and Larry then drove me to my home —I remembered that it was just about 6:30 in the morning. Debbie was up, happy to have me home, and eager to hear about the trip. I remember telling her a few details from our story and then collapsing into bed.

Thinking about the journey, I was glad I didn't back off on Sunday at the airport and say, "I'm not taking a chance. Good luck, guys." Now I realized that the trip, though truncated and disappointing in some ways, had been worth it. We had had our differences about going on, but in the end had pretty much come together. And through it all, Larry and Kevin had kept us laughing and given us hope. I thought of the van ride home, even the fact that we had the van, and Larry's dialing in on Lewis Black to keep us laughing, his finding Ralph's and the culinary experience that fortified us, and then his driving shift getting us into New York, and finally Kevin's turn bringing the van home. I thought again of Randal Patrick McMurphy in *Cuckoo's Nest* leading the men from the mental institution out to sea and letting them experience it all. Florence had come close to totally shutting us down, but Larry and Kevin had encouraged us to get the most out of the experience, and we had, and then they led us out of there and home. In the end, Florence was not as cruel to Myrtle Beach as was predicted — she caused power outages, flood damage, but no great structural damages.

As I think about the trip from my easy chair at home, I can still see Larry's smile when he said, "Man, what a front nine. I one-putted six holes."

Leatherstocking

It was turning out to be a great week in Cooperstown. The AP English Literature summer course at Cooperstown High School surpassed my expectations with a professor who knew his stuff and had an excellent sense of humor. My lodging was two blocks from the Baseball Hall of Fame, and I had had a chance to visit the Baseball Mecca Tuesday afternoon. Wednesday night had been thrilling though challenging, for I had attended a black tie fund raiser at the Fenimore Art Museum dressed in shorts and a polo shirt, and been allowed to stand in a corner out of sight, so that I could hear Professor Arthur Rampersad speak about Jackie Robinson, a hero of mine. This afternoon we were out of the AP class at 2:30, and I had gotten a 3:45 tee time at a course I had longed to play for years, the Leatherstocking Golf Course. I even had visions of seeing along the edge of the fairways the ghosts of Natty Bumppo and Chingachook, characters from Cooper's *The Deerslayer*, a novel I had read in graduate school. I had always felt a surge of adrenaline when I was near a world that imaginary characters have roamed. I arrived at the golf course brimming with excitement, signed in, and was ready.

. . . . .

I look around and then step quickly to the first tee of — yes, the Leatherstocking Golf Course. The four guys ahead of me, who have a cooler in the back of one of their carts, are well out of my range. With the easy late afternoon sun lighting the course up, I am in heaven thinking about the opportunity to play this course on my own. My game has been coming together slowly, and I love the chance to hit two or three balls if no one is behind me. I reach down to place my tee on Hole One.

"Hey, fella," a shout from the starter's hut. "I got someone to join up with you."

"Shit," I grumble, "I wanted this course to myself today" as a little shorter but older version of Seattle Mariner's Randy Johnson emerges from behind the hut, and I step away from the tee box toward him extending my hand, "Paul," I say, last names not being part of the protocol when strangers are matched up on the links. "John," he says and he grips my hand firmly, even though his whole long, gangly body looks very loosely connected.

"Go ahead, you were about ready to hit."

"Thanks," I say, looking for the approximate place I had selected earlier. "I've never played this course before," I add.

"Play here three times a week, if I can," he says. "It's a good course, a few challenging holes. I remember the first time I played here — didn't even know where to hit the ball, but now I know the course pretty good. I'll show you."

"Well, happy you joined me," I say and mean it. I look out, pretty straight away, 322 from the white, with an elevated green, bunkers in the front and on both sides. I make good contact and send the ball pretty straight about 200 yards.

As John approaches the tee, he adjusts his golf hat which is almost too big, even with his long hair. His white and grey golf shirt is loose, and his dark grey shorts — definitely not golf shorts — stop just below his muscled thighs. Loose grey socks rise out of his well-worn Reebok sneakers.

And he is left-handed — Randy Johnson again. He doesn't waste any time setting up, and with lighting speed, he swings the club and sends the ball a mile high, ending up twenty yards or so ahead of me.

He's walking and carrying a bag, and I have a cart because frankly I wanted the advantage today of really enjoying the game and not have to worry about dragging my butt once I hit the back nine.

"Want to jump in," I say, and John says, "No, I'm all right. I need to walk, and they don't like it if you ride in someone's cart without paying." I never quite understand the reasoning there, since I already paid, but I don't pursue the topic. "Maybe later, on the hills," he says.

I bogey the first hole and so does John, missing a thirty foot putt by inches. Hole two looks tight to me, 372 from the white with pine trees on both right and left. The green in the distance, another one rising up, looks small with a sand trap off the left side. I tee off and hit a slice to the right that catches a pine tree and drops down.

"I've been there a few times," John says in a good-natured way. He steps up and lashes one down the center, this time much lower and much farther. It's pretty clear to me that he not only knows the course well, but he also has a pretty good game.

I drive my cart near him as we head out. "Live around here, John?"

"About ten miles away."

"Is this vacation week for you?"

"Sort of."

I look out on Otsego Lake and see a sailboat with four smaller boats trailing, a sailing lesson it appears.

"What's your line of work?" I ask.

"Cement. Factory not too far from here. You?"

"Teacher. I'm taking a course at Cooperstown High School. Summer program."

"Whadda ya teach?" he asks.

"English. Summer program is in Advanced Placement English."

"Not sure I know what that's about," he says.

"Well, it's sort of a college type course in high school. Kids can take it for college credit. Course gives us ideas about how to teach AP."

"Oh," John says.

I am starting to enjoy John as a companion on this golf outing. He has a way of giving little pieces of advice about, for example, the choice of club in tight situations or how to position your body on a slope. And I sense he knows that advice given is rarely executed well, but he seems to have a generous heart. We are on the seventh hole, and I am on my third shot. John on his second, when he signals me. "Paul, come over here. I want to show you something." I drive the golf cart over in his direction and stop. He is pointing at something on the ground. I get out and walk over. It's a plaque with some writing on it.

"Johnny Bench, a 346 yard drive in 1992 at the Hall of Fame Classic."

"That is incredible," I say, looking back down the hill to the tee. "And it's uphill too."

"They say he was one hell of a golfer, shot a 65 a couple of years later at the Classic."

"Imagine if he had taken up golf instead of baseball," I say, and I look back to the tee at seven again.

. . . . .

On the tee of the ninth, I look up through a narrow gap into nothing but distant sky and trees. "I have no idea where I'm going here," I say. John walks over and points at a particular towering pine in the distance. "Aim for that tree," he says, "and maybe from this distance — about 160 and uphill — I would go with a four iron." I am holding a five in my hand, but I trust John and slip it back in my bag and reach for a four.

My ball had gone relatively straight before disappearing over the rise. The hill is on the steep side, and John is walking nearby and laboring a bit. "Mind if I jump on now," he says. I give him a thumbs up, and he straps his clubs onto the cart and jumps aboard.

When we level out at the top of the hill, I see our two golf balls, his about 5 feet from the green, mine about 30 feet to the left of the green. 'Not bad," I say and he laughs.

We have teed off on the tenth, and I am curious about something John had said when we started. "You said you were sort of on vacation earlier?"

"Well, I'm on disability leave."

I take a sip of water. "Injury at the factory?"

John seems to be staring at the Fenimore Cooper Museum, and then he turns slowly back, "I uhh, well, about three years ago, I had a kidney removed — cancer." He pauses on the word and the whole course seems to be still. We have reached his ball, but he does not get out of the cart. "See, I had been urinating blood for a while and my doctor kept giving me medicine for it. But one day at work, I went in to take a piss, and a huge clot came out and exploded in the urinal. When they took out the kidney, it was the size of a softball."

"God," I say looking over at John, who is now staring straight ahead.

"Well, they said they got it, and I started to feel better. And then last year, I went to the emergency room because my asthma was acting up. The doctor there said I needed an X-Ray." He paused.

"Trouble," I say softly.

"Dark spots on both my lungs — a lot of them. It had spread."

"Could they operate?"

"Too many. So now I'm on alternative medicines and watching my diet. I used to weigh about 220. Now I'm about 160." We both stare at the green ahead. "You know, it's really my wife. Well, she's my second wife — quite a bit younger. We got two kids, one three and one six. She says this isn't going to beat us. She has even made a contact with a doctor in Mexico for some new drug. She's a hell of a woman." He pauses again and breathes very deeply.

"Hey," slapping the top of the cart with his right hand. "Let's go for the green. I'd use a seven iron from here."

On the back nine his shots have become more and more accurate, perhaps helped a bit by the energy he would have used up walking. I smile and think, "Hey, I am helping John's game."

I have to ask though I already have a sense of his answer, "What keeps you going, John?"

"My wife, my two kids," and for a moment there is silence, and then he looks at me and says, "And you know what. I really like this game of golf."

· · · · ·

I can't see the flag on fifteen, and John shouts from where he has just hit the ball. "Aim for the target in the tree, about a six iron." At first, I don't see anything, and then a black and white bull's eye leaps out at me in the distance about fifty feet up in a tree. I take John's advice. I grab my six iron and make fairly good contact. When we go over the hill, I see that my ball is about forty feet from the green. I get on with my next shot, just miss the putt as my ball rolls by the hole, and then sink it for a bogey, but I feel very good about the hole.

From a postage stamp of a tee, I look out across Otsego Lake. The fairway at its nearest distance I estimate is about 130 yards. Then the Lake cuts into the land, and the distance jumps dramatically. The temptation is to try to get the ball on the par five down the fairway more. I hear John's voice, "No sense taking a chance here. You just want to get across the water."

He is right, and I take my five iron and make solid contact — it lands about twenty yards inland from the water.

I arrive on the green first. John shanked his second shot and has spent some time along the water looking for it before he dropped a ball. He had wanted to walk the last hole, maybe to avoid any discussions with the starter, but maybe because he needed to for himself. He is moving slowly, and his shadow lengthens out behind him. I putt out, and John picks up his ball after missing a long putt.

"It was good playing with you, Paul," he says extending his hand. I reach out and shake his hand.

"Glad we had this chance," I say.

Walking to my car, I think of John heading back to his wife and two kids, and I hope that he has more time with them and more time to play this game he loves.

I Was Scared

"When I have fears that I may cease to be ..." the poet says, but I do not think so much of my demise as I do of those paralyzing fears that played and continue to play such a strong role in my life. I believe that so much of my fear is because of an overactive imagination, conjuring up worlds that menace and terrify. That my mind even contains worlds so dark and terrifying I can't figure out, but I do know that at times the fear has been powerful and immobilizing. In looking back now, I am not sure how much fear has contributed to the direction of my life, but I know that the fears were forces that sometimes gripped me tightly.

I am sitting on a sloped floor in a room the shape of a square box, the right side of my body against a wall. My arms wrap around my knees, and I try to be low and inconspicuous, but all that I am sure of is that the other walls are getting closer, and the ceiling is dropping down slowly. Everything is coming in, getting tighter, and I see no way out. "Dad!" I yell. "Dad! Dad!" I am in my bedroom in the farmhouse on the Cooksborough Road where I spent my first few years. I hear rustling, voices, a light, and then the floors creak as my father walks down the hallway and then opens my nearly shut door.

"What's going on?" he says calmly, as he stands in the doorway.

"I'm not sure. It was like I was in this room that kept getting smaller, and I felt trapped, and I shouted your name, and then I woke up."

"You feel ok now," he says, moving closer.

"I guess so."

"Well," now standing over me and speaking calmly, "probably just a bad dream. You should be ok. Try to get back to sleep." As he starts to turn, he says, "I'm going down to the kitchen and have some tea. If you need me, just call."

Going to the kitchen was a good thing for me because the grating in the floor allowed the kitchen light to come into my room, and the light made me feel safer. Dad was down there.

. . . . .

The moment I trace my "official" claustrophobia to, however, happened years later. I am in the back seat of my brother's car, a Toyota. My older brother Leo is driving, and my younger brother John is the passenger in the front seat. We have crossed the bridge over the stream that runs through his property outside the village of Tomhannock. Ahead of us leading to his small house is not really a road, but a pathway on grass that cars have worn down a bit. The road swings a bit left, and then you follow a circular path to the main entrance of the house. Parked near the house is a car that we do not recognize.

We are about twenty yards from the house, when three men, one after the other, exit the door of the house, and each is carrying a shotgun. My hand instinctively reaches for the door handle, but there is none. I have forgotten that my brother's car is a two-door. My heart is pounding and my whole body stiffens.

"What is this," Leo says, and then, "Ah, what do you know, it's Bobby Stanton."

I now see clearly that the last guy out is Bobby, and I breathe in and exhale slowly. The Stanton family were long-time friends of my brother's, and Leo had told them where the key was in case they ever wanted to use the place. It was hunting season, and Bobby had taken advantage of the house in the country to use as a base of operation for a day. But the moment for me was terrifying.

From that day on, I was subject to the fear of confined spaces, especially in theaters, on planes, and in certain vehicles that had no back door or door I could reach.

Two moments come to mind: I am in New York City with my wife and a good friend. Jeff and I have left Debbie in her downstate office in the South Tower of the World Trade Center. We have tickets to see a matinee performance of the thriller *Death Trap*. I am already tense when we reach the theater because Jeff is a big guy, 6' 3" and pushing 300 pounds. He needs the aisle seat. When we reach our seats, orchestra level about 15 rows from the stage, I go in first. The seat next to me is empty, and the rest of the row is occupied. There is not much space in front of me, and I notice that Jeff has already extended his legs into the aisle. But the seat next to me is empty, and it is the key to getting me through this thriller. "Please, Lord," I say to myself, "let this seat remain empty."

The theater lights have dimmed when I hear some commotion to my left, and Jeff is forcing himself up from his ensconced position. He steps back, and I see a short, but quite rotund middle-aged woman who whispers, "Excuse me, please." I stand up to let her pass by me, and she settles down into the empty seat next to me. I am trapped. I am not sure how I will be able to overcome the panic of this situation. One trick that helps me is holding my hands like blinders on the sides of my face to block out what my peripheral vision would reveal. I also try to compress my body as much as possible, and I, thank God, have the help of the play, which is a genuine thriller. But a close call.

A closer call came just before a plane flight from Chicago after attending the graduation of my nephew from De-Paul University. Knowing my psychological needs, my wife always pays careful attention when she books a flight, especially regarding aisle seats. I hear her behind me talking to the flight attendant, "I don't think these seats are going to work," she says with that strength of voice I know so well. When I see the seats, middle and window, I know it will be one bad ride.

Debbie says, "Let me take the window," and she climbs in and sits down. As soon as I sit in the middle, I know I am in trouble, "I don't think I can do it."

At that moment the aisle passenger shows up — I knew it would be a big guy — well over 6 feet and on the heavy side. He must sense something because he says, "You two ok?" Debbie responds, "My husband has a problem with claustrophobia and though I arranged for an aisle seat, we didn't get one." In a flash, the guy says, "Hey, I love the window seat — let me climb in, and you two move over." We get up to let him into the window seat, and I say, "You don't know how much this means — I really appreciate it." He smiles and utters the phrase that sometimes drives me nuts, "No problem," but he adds, "Happy to help out." In this case, the phrase "No problem" was the sweetest sound.

· · · · ·

Living in the country has its wonderful pluses — fresh air, open spaces, serenity. The flip side is isolation, loneliness, and darkness. Until I set off for college, I lived in the country for the first six years on a farm on the Cooksborough Road and for the next twelve, at the south end of Raymertown, a small village. I have described in my book *Voices from Room 6* the traumatic experience I suffered at the age of 8 when a stranger asked me if I wanted a ride to our country store in Raymertown, my intended walking destination. A series of questions in a car that didn't move for what seemed eternity and then a miraculous release with the words, "See you again some day, Paul." I was free, and my mother heard it all as I told my story through sobs and tears and gasping.

In our house, my brother John and I slept in a small room at the top of the stairs. The position of my bed allowed me to look out into the hallway. When I did, I would look past the sleeping figure of my brother on the left side of the room. When he was asleep — he entered another zone — there was no hope of discussing what I was seeing on the walls at the top of the stairs. They were in the house, more than one — burglars, killers, escaped convicts — they had come up the stairs and were now in the other two rooms on the second floor. Just waiting, just biding their time to do the inevitable. They had moved stealthily up the stairs — I had seen their reflections on the walls as cars passed by on Route 7, the highway leading up into the mountains of Vermont.

My hope was in one word — "Dad!" I yelled. "Dad!" I yelled louder. John twisted and turned and then went back to sleep, but there was hope. I could hear the rustling and the murmuring between my mother and my father. And then the light over the stairway and hall went on, and I heard him climbing the stairs. "What's going on?" he said, his wide frame in the middle of the doorway.

"There are some men in the house, I saw them."

Patiently my father said, "Oh, uhh, where are they?"

"They have to be in Leo's and Rose's rooms," I said. "Yes, they were moving that way."

My father turned and walked down the hall. I could hear him switch the light on, a long pause, and then light off, and the same pattern in the room across the hall.

"I think we have taken care of the problem, There is no one there."

"You sure, Dad?"

"Yup, I checked. It's ok. Try to get some sleep."

As the hall light went off, I trusted that my Dad had taken care of the menace, and just to be safe, I turned toward the wall, and not out into the hallway, where I might see someone else sneak up the stairs with the purpose of … well, perhaps murdering me.

Many years later, I experienced a night which would send my students into shock when I would tell the story. "You would do that?" they exclaimed. The story goes like this: After my father died and before my mother moved into an apartment — maybe a period of four months — my siblings and I would take turns staying overnight with my mother, who was still mentally very sharp, but who had been worn down by severe arthritis. On this particular night, it was my turn and I had stayed up quite late watching television. Let me say right off that though we lived in a small village, our house was a good distance — maybe a couple of football fields from the neighbors. As the evening wore on, I became more and more conscious of possible strangers coming to the door — I kept the front spotlight on. Before heading up to bed, I checked all the locks carefully. In the stillness, my mother's snoring reigned.

Upstairs, I slept in one of the bedrooms in the front known as Leo's room. The bed in that room was a double bed as opposed to my old single bed in the room at the top of the stairs. My oldest brother had been away a number of my younger years studying for the priesthood, but when he was home, this room was his. It had two windows, one looking out at Route 7, the other looking out over the porch roof at our driveway which slowly bent to the left past a barn featuring a Wolf's Head Oil sign and then out to Route 7. On this particular night, I took out a cigar that I had found in a desk drawer downstairs, a remnant of my father's smoking days. The light was off on this warm summer night, and I had the window open to blow the smoke out and to catch a little breeze. Maybe half way through the cigar, I heard the rumble of what sounded like cycles — and then the roar grew louder — and suddenly they were out at the end of our driveway — three cyclists. They cut their engines, and then one guy's curses lit up the night. "Son of a bitch — I thought that damn rattle would stop — you guys must have heard it — God Damn.. Yeah, there it is — the fender has come loose — I must have lost the fucking nut."

I had carefully moved back out of the window and pressed the lit end of the cigar into an old saucer that had been used to hold a plant. Their voices were coming across like idling cycles — and then I heard the fateful words — "I gotta make a fucking call — I'm going to have to knock on the door of this house. Come on, let's give it a shot."

My mind was racing — "Ok, they reach the front door, I will have time to get out. Mom will take so long getting to the door that I can open the screen, hit the roof, drop down, and take off. I'd be gone by the time Mom opens the door."

Then, "Wait, I got a crazy idea," one of the cyclists said, "My belt, I can run it under the fender and up around the seat — I think it might work." I prayed while he attempted his primitive solution. "Son of a bitch, Bob, that might do it. Son of a bitch."

And then the sweetest sounds of all — the engines kicking over, and the best sound of all, the motorcycles roaring into the night.

"You would have taken off and left your Mom?" the students, almost in choral effect, would cry.

"At least one would survive," I would respond. I think in their heart and soul, they felt I never would have left my mother to the fate of the three cyclists. In the end, they were probably right, but for a moment....

· · · · ·

And then there were the movies and television. I remember so well a moment when my sister took me to a movie in the old Troy Cinema. I don't remember the title of the movie and too much of what it was about, except that it was a Western. But the moment I will never forget is this: the bad guy, at least his outfit and the music told me so, started walking right toward the camera, which I realized in later years was the point of view of the "good guy" in the movie, but for me the bad guy was walking right toward me, and I remember feeling so scared, and saying to my sister as I grabbed her arm, "He's going to get me." I remember her saying something like, "Don't worry — it's only a movie."

The two monster movies that scared me when I was a few years older were *The Beast from Twenty Thousand Fathoms* and *Them*. *Them* was scarier because of one thing I was to realize over time: the longer you keep hidden what is causing the acts of horror or the mayhem, the scarier the movie is. *Them* kept showing clues of how bad it was — the mutilated bodies, the huge footprints, but the audience didn't see the monster until near the end. As we would experience again with the movie *Jaws* many years later.

That movie truth may have been what made *Suspense Theater*, a 50's television show, so scary. The terrible suspense building in me was caused, a realization that would come in time, by the narrator's deep and somber voice and carefully dropped clues that were inserted into the story so well that the actual revelation or climax was often not equal to the power of the fear felt as the story developed.

I am always perplexed at the ability of some people to see the most horrifying shows and come out with an understatement like, "Not bad" or "Ahhhhh — ok." I sometimes think that they have some sensors missing in their brains that signal, "You should be scared out of your mind right NOW."

The conversation had turned to horror films in my classroom. "Mr. O'Brien, have you ever seen *Manhunter*?" a student asked. I said that I hadn't, and he added, "If you want scary, that is the film for you. You got to check it out." I offered that I didn't want scary, and therefore that it was not the film for me. He countered, "Come on, give it a try. I have the DVD at home." I shook my head, "Sorry, Ray, don't want to see it. I have a problem with horror films."

The next day, the film was on my desk, and the class watched as I picked it up and looked at it. "Ray, I told you I am not a guy for scary horror films." He smiled and said,

"Ok, just take it home, put it on your coffee table, and if you have a few moments where you feel brave, give it a whirl."

I took the movie home, and it sat on the table near the television for a few days. On a Friday afternoon, I got home early. Debbie and I were planning to go out to dinner that night, and so I decided that I should do some stationary biking. before the big feast. I looked at the film, picked it up, and said, "Well, I can stop it if it's too much."

On the stationary bike, I lasted about 20 minutes before I ejected the video. A character by the name of Will Graham was investigating the murder of a family, and what was terrifying for me was the fact that he was going through the rooms of the house imagining that he was the killer, putting himself in the place of the killer. It's in the dark, flashlights shining, children moving and looking back at the one with the light. The killer. It was really bad.

I did not touch the video again until the following Tuesday. I got on the bike and with Debbie still an hour from arriving home, I decided to watch another segment — maybe 20 minutes. The scare factor remained very high. In this segment, Graham reached out to Dr. Hannibal Lecter, with whom he had already established a dark relationship, for assistance in the pursuit of the criminal. I got off the bike more tense than I was after the previous viewing.

At school I was teased by the student who had loaned me the video. I said to him, "I am not sure that I can finish it, but I may give it one more shot." I did, and the suspense, tension, and terror in me lifted substantially because the director made a decision to show the viewer the murderer. And though the "serial killer" was a freaky character and still menacing, the issue of the unknown was lifted. It did have one of those endings — "Will the good guy make it in time?" — but I made it to the end.

The problem was, however, that I had been set up. I had met Dr. Hannibal Lecter, and I knew what he was capable of, so when *Silence of the Lambs,* starring Jodie Foster as Clarice Starling, an FBI student in training, and Anthony Hopkins as Dr. Hannibal Lecter (previously played by Brian Cox), opened to great reviews, the trap had been set. Fear vs the desire to see a great flick.

The movie was playing at the Northway Cinema off Central Avenue. On three different occasions, I had driven to the theater to see the film, and, unable to rise above the fear that gripped me, I had driven away. On the fourth try — a snow day from school, which allowed me to be there for the early show — I was determined. In the lobby I sat on a bench some distance away from the ticket booth. I was about forty percent in favor of seeing the film, still tipped to the side of walking out and driving away. And then they walked in. An old couple, the man's arm sort of guiding his wife along. They passed me, I nodded to them, and they nodded back. When they reached the ticket booth, I heard, "Two seniors for *Silence of the Lambs*." I couldn't believe my ears — there were five other movies playing, and they had chosen *Silence of the Lambs*. I turned and watched them through the glass wall, as they approached the concession station. "If they can do it, you can do it!" I reassured myself.

"One adult," I said.

"For which movie?"

"Uhh, ahhh, *Silence*."

"One for *Silence of the Lambs*," he announced.

I never skip popcorn, but this day I did. I was too tense to, as Frank McCourt would say of America's odd choice of words, "consume" popcorn. When I entered the theater for the movie, I could see the old couple about 10 rows down on the left. I approached them slowly.

"Excuse me, please," I sort of whispered.

The man's hand was in the popcorn box as he looked up at me, "Yes, can I help you?"

"I would like to ask a favor of you, if you don't mind. This movie has me really scared, and it hasn't even started. If it's ok, can I sit across the aisle from you? Having someone near me would make me feel safer."

He smiled, though his wife look puzzled, "You sit right there, young man," pointing at the seat directly across from them. "You'll be all right."

"I really appreciate that," I said and took the seat he had pointed to.

There were probably four or five moments that entered my terror zone: meeting Lecter for the first time was riveting and terrifying at the same time because you see the mind of Lecter at work. Clarice has come to talk with him in the mental hospital for the criminally insane with the hopes of getting some clues to a serial killer the FBI is pursuing. Hopkins' portrayal of the character is so dark and so menacing — his insights into Clarice as she faces him through the bars are demonic. As she leaves the hospital after the interview, the old fella across the aisle looked over and quietly said, "You okay?" I gave him a thumbs-up.

Another high moment of shock and terror was when Lecter fools the guards, kills them and escapes — back to the old "He is out there motif." Another look, another thumbs-up. And then for a split second, there is a connection that flashes in my brain. My father in the room when I was in terror, and how his presence calmed things.

When Clarice enters the basement where the serial killer has descended, my whole body was rigid with fear. Of course, before she goes down into the dark basement, I implore her, "Clarice, do not go down there. He is there, and he will kill you." After all, this is a guy who flays women out of a desire to make a woman's suit from skin. She descends — and I remember twisting and turning in my seat as if I were Clarice just barely staying out of the reach of the killer.

At the end, the writer and movie director did not let me off the terror hook, for Dr. Hannibal Lecter is still out there. He makes a phone call to Clarice, which ends with his request that she not pursue him, and then his words, "I am having an old friend for dinner."

I walked out with the old couple and thanked them for helping me get through the movie. He laughed, and his wife laughed too. Then she said, "You know, young man, I can understand why you wanted to be near us. That movie really was scary."

In looking back at the experience of seeing *Silence of the Lambs,* I began to think about the role of art, in this case an outstanding film, in helping me to come to terms with my fears. In the end I made the choice to see the film, and I did rely to a degree on the nearby support of the elderly couple, but the film's brilliant direction and acting helped me to see into new regions of darkness and evil and how one both confronts it and copes with it. In a way, I was Clarice entering the terrible darkness and emerging wiser and more aware of humankind.

· · · · ·

Still, fear will always play a part of my life. I haven't really talked about the fear of losing loved ones suddenly and tragically — and that has happened. I remember taking our beloved three-legged cat CT to the vet and discovering that he had cancer. There seemed to be hope, but then the day of the surgery to remove the growth, we got a call that the cancer had spread to his lungs, and it was just a matter of time. I feared the final moment, and it was difficult, watching the injection that took his life. Nor have I spoken of that fear when a cough does not go away — I did smoke for eleven years, especially when you watch the testimonials of people who should have stopped smoking and didn't stop and later realized it was too late.

Late at night at Raquette Lake, when Debbie and I are the only ones in the house on the North Bay and she is sound asleep, my imagination does go to work. Thinking of a motorcycle gang seeking help in the night or someone in the woods who has escaped from Dannemora, a maximum security prison in the North Country — it happened, you know — and we WERE at Raquette during the fugitive period. The slightest sound tells me someone with skill is jimmying the lock. They are down there. The circular staircase leading up to our bedroom will be a momentary challenge if they don't have a light. I think of running out on the landing and throwing stuff down the staircase, but no, it's too late — so how much stuff can we get up against the door in a few seconds: dresser, chair, fan, suitcase. And then making a sheet rope tying together the two sheets so that Debbie and I can escape — damn, the car keys are on the nail downstairs — well, into the woods before they realize we are gone.

No one appreciates the light of dawn more than I do.

College Freshmen Year: Five Lessons

Arrival

With the exception of two two-week summer sessions at Camp Tekakwitha, when I was in seventh and eighth grades, I had never been away from home for more than an overnight. When my parents drove me down one Sunday morning to Iona College in New Rochelle to begin my four years of college, I could feel the sense of separation building. They helped me get settled in my off-campus house on Mayflower Avenue, and then we went down to the College Diner on North Avenue for lunch. I remember during lunch that it was hard to talk and very hard to swallow food. Neither of my parents had had the opportunity to go to college, and these trips with their children were special. I recalled how exciting it was to be awakened in the darkness and setting out with my parents to visit my brother Leo in Rochester, Baltimore, and Washington, D.C., the cities he studied in on his eight year journey to become a priest. And how our hearts would constrict when we were saying good-bye to him to head home.

After a lunch filled with a forced and unnatural conversation, they drove me back up Mayflower to my house, and we all got out of the car to say good-bye. I remember my Dad, tears welling up in his eyes, giving me a hand-shake, and saying something very simple like "Do good." My Mom gave me a hug and looked at me. She said words that seemed so natural for her, "Be a good boy."

I held the door for Mom as she got in the car, and then I stepped back, "Bye," I said. And then my hands went to my forehead, my index fingers pressing against my eyebrows to hold the tears back. I stepped back and watched my father put the car in drive, pull out, and then take a right onto Faneuil Place, and they were gone. The tears came down as I made my way to the steps of the porch on the front of the house. I sat down, feeling that awful ache you get in your heart when you feel a loved one's absence.

"Hi," a voice had broken through my ache. I looked up and saw a handsome, young Asian man. "My name is John, and I live in this house. I assume you are the new student who was supposed to arrive today." He held out his hand.

"Hello," I said, offering my hand. "I'm Paul — ahhh, my parents just left a little while ago, and I guess I'm feeling a little sorry for myself."

John gave me a warm smile. "You'll be ok," he said, sitting down next to me. "It takes a little time."

"How long have you been here?" I asked.

"This is my second year," John said.

"You like the college?"

"Yes, I've adjusted pretty well."

"Tough leaving your home and your parents?" I asked.

"Yes, they couldn't afford to come to America. We said good-bye at the Hong Kong airport."

"Wow," I said, "and first time in America?"

"Oh yes, me and my one suitcase, but a good thing, we have relatives who lived in the Bronx, so I stayed with them a couple of days, and they drove me up here to find an apartment. And I met Mrs. Tesseraro." He smiled. "You will like her. She's good to us."

"That's nice," I said. "Lot to get used to. I am nervous about the classes too. School been good for you? I mean, you doing ok with grades?"

He laughed, "Yeah, I do ok, but I work hard, and I plan my time very carefully. Actually, I have a few jobs, so I can't afford to waste time."

"Any advice for someone just getting started?"

"Ah yes, I do," — he spoke so clearly, enunciating each word. "There is a temptation among new guys — I saw it last year — to go out nights to parties or just to drink — in New Rochelle, it's the Village Inn and the Beechmont. Don't do it. Stay in nights and study. On the weekends, maybe one night for partying but not two. So much hinges on the way you start your first year. I really mean that. Don't go out — fight the temptation."

I looked at him and said, "Thanks, John."

· · · · ·

"O'BRIEN! O'BRIEN!" I rolled out of my single bed and went to my third floor window that looked out on May-flower Avenue. I looked down at five "moons" — rear-ends announcing that I was a loser for staying in and studying, five "moons" of five other freshmen. These Mayflower moons appeared a number of times during that fall semester, all from my first year friends at the college.

John's admonition and his incredible routines, however, were models for me. I couldn't equal the intensity of what he did — the balance of academics and work (four jobs), but once I settled in and got a grip on my studies, I was able to take on a few little jobs, one working with John in the Admissions Office of the College.

Of the six to seven regulars who walked down Mayflower Avenue to indulge in life at the Village Inn and the Beechmont, only one survived the first year of college. My friend Bill from Camden made it a year and a half before he dropped out. John remained a good friend, often coming home with me on college breaks and fitting in nicely with our family. A guiding light for three years, he graduated Summa Cum Laude and entered Georgetown Medical School. After medical school we fell out of touch, but often I think of him and remember that first meeting on the porch steps and realize how fortunate I was to begin my college days with someone like John.

Inebriated

John Ng was a light during my first year in college, but I do remember one occasion when I entered a dark world, probably aided by the fact that John was working as a waiter in China Town that night and often stayed over with good friends; if he had been at our house and seen the gathering and drinking prior to our departure, I would have gotten a "what are you doing" look. New Rochelle College (All Women) was having a mixer with Iona (All Men) on a Saturday night, and a group of us decided to go. In those days, the drinking age was 18, and we, as young men do on occasions, decided to have a few drinks before the dance.

It started in the crowded little kitchen of our boarding house on Mayflower Avenue. Tony set a bottle of Southern Comfort on the table — "There you go, boys. Janis Joplin's favorite drink. Enjoy."

We took turns pouring the drink into our glasses.

"Oh boy," Bobby said, "this is sweet stuff."

"Oh man, it goes down so smoothly," Bill added.

"Give me another touch," Gene said to Bill who was still holding the bottle.

I agreed that it was sweet, but I needed another shot to make sure I was right and taking the bottle from Bill, I poured a little more into my glass. "To you, Tony," I said, lifting my glass, "for introducing us to Janis Joplin's world."

Tony laughed and then said, "Ok, guys, here's the deal. We hit the Beechmont for another round and then, 'Girls, look out, here come the dancing Gaels."

The Beechmont, located across the street from Iona College, was a popular bar for students. When we arrived about 8:00 or so, the place was fairly crowded, but we managed to grab one of the few remaining tables. "I owe you one from last week, Paulie," Bobby said, "what are ya drinking?"

I didn't hesitate, "Seven and Seven," I said, my favorite mixed drink. Tony plopped down in the chair next to me holding a bottle of Bud. "We probably got time for a couple of rounds," he said. "Dance is from 8:00 to 11:00 — get there maybe in 9:00 range, don't want to rush these babes too hard. Got your dancing shoes on tonight, Paulie?"

I laughed and said, "Oh, I am ready," as Bobby handed me my drink. The truth of the matter — I was one of those guys who helped to support the walls of whatever dancing venue we were in. I sipped the drink, "Ahh, very nice, thanks, Bobby." He lifted his rum and coke in a toast and glanced back at a few young women who had decided to stand next to their table and dance.

"Got to be on our best behavior tonight," Bill said. "Those Ursuline nuns will be out in force to protect their women. Don't get too carried away on the dance floor."

"Gets a little heated, and they will step in between you and your dancing partner," Gene added.

"I'm so quick," Tony said, "that when they try to step in, I'll be dancing with another girl."

· · · · ·

We had another round and then set out for the College of New Rochelle, actually only a ten minute drive away. The dance was in the gym, and as we entered the building, we hesitated for a second. The entrance way to the dance floor was between two tables, each one with a nun standing right behind it. The taller nun with a serious expression looked familiar, but I couldn't recall the context. We had consumed mints on the way over, and three of us had smoked a cigarette, so we were confident that our imbibing would not be an issue.

"Paul O'Brien, Iona College," I said. The tall nun stared at me, then nodded, and gestured for me to enter the gym. Stepping forward, my eye caught a policeman off to my right seated at a small table watching the admissions.

The lights were down though not as far down as some of us would have liked, the music was revved up pretty well — orchestrated by a DJ on the stage of the gym/auditorium, and the girls were on the floor, mainly dancing with each other. Tony had already stepped out and was into a dance with a girl who seemed as outgoing as he. We applauded them briefly and then moved on, Gene and I heading to the soda and pretzel/chip table, and Bill and Bobby moving out in search. I picked up a cola and then stepped back to observe the scene, while Gene started talking to a girl behind the refreshment table.

I wasn't sure whether it was the beat of the music or the lights the DJ began flashing, but I felt kind of light-headed, though my legs and feet and body started to move with the music, "Yeah," I began to sing along, "I Want to Hold Your Hand." I don't even remember setting my soda down, but I was out on the floor, dancing with two girls who were both very good. They smiled when they saw me join, and maybe were just being overly nice, but they let me have fun dancing with them. The fact of the matter is that I rarely ever danced — once or twice at our high school dances, and that was only to a few slow songs and feebly to the song "Splish Splash" by Bobby Darin — mainly because a friend had taught me prior to the dance a few basic moves to that song.

And we kept dancing — I do remember "That's What I Want" and the rest were a blur — good dancing songs, but the one I remember vividly was "Moon River." One of the girls had backed away when the song began, and I started dancing with the other one. As I looked out over her shoulder, the bright lights of the word BATH ROOM in a distant hallway began pulsating — and I knew in my soul that the BATH ROOM was my destination. I stepped back, looked at the girl, and said, "Excuse me." She seemed confused and gave me an odd expression, but I had my focus. If I put one foot out and then the other very carefully, I might have a chance to reach the distant BATH ROOM.

I saw three booths, entered the middle one, and threw up in the toilet. After I flushed the toilet, my head began spinning — I reached over, locked the door, and collapsed back on the toilet.

Meanwhile, my friends were having a good time, until someone, I think it was Gene, noticed that I was not around. He mentioned it to Bill, who told Gene to check the bathroom. There were a couple other recessed areas that the guys checked. Someone asked the nuns if anyone had stepped outside, and one of the nuns said, "If you leave, you don't return." Gene had reported back that the only one in the bathroom was a guy having a number two. Bill decided to check for himself, stood up on the toilet in the next booth and peered over — "Paulie, Paulie, whatcha doing, Paulie?"

The policeman, whom I had seen at the table on arrival, was looking straight into my eyes, "Listen, pal," he said. "I will move back a few steps, and then I will have you walk to me ... when I tell you to walk. Understand?" I nodded. Bill stood to the side with a little grin on his face, but Gene who had just come in looked tense.

The officer walked about ten steps backwards, adjacent to the sinks. "Ok," he said, "walk." On my second step I swayed to the right and almost went down. "OK, buddy," he moved toward me and grabbed my arm. "I am going to give you about 30 minutes in here, and then your two friends are going to escort you out of this building." He then looked at Bill, " You said you have a car, correct." Bill nodded. "Ok," the policeman said, while squeezing my arm harder, "listen, you, your two buddies are going to take you home. Look at me, if there is any problem getting out, if the Good Sister has to call me over because you have fallen down or something, I will take you in tonight and book you, understand? Do you understand?" I nodded.

Sometimes, it's good to have teamwork. Tonight we clicked. Bobby and Tony engaged one of the nuns in conversation as Bill, Gene, and I walked by — each one discretely holding me up by my arms, while my eyes were fixed on the door leading outside.

On the ride back, Tony said, "Jesus, he only had a little of this," and held the empty bottle of Southern Comfort next to my nose. Thank God, I was at the window. I barely had it half rolled down when I threw up out the window.

"Come onnnn, O'Brien," Bill said, "have some mercy on my car."

Bill and Gene escorted me up to the third floor, and Bill helped me get into bed. As my head hit the pillow, Bill leaned over and said, "Good Night, Paulie. Remember, stay away from that Southern Comfort."

In the middle of Sunday afternoon, I was sitting in our kitchen having a cup of tea when John Ng arrived home. He walked into the kitchen, smiled, and said, "How was your dance?" I smiled back and said, "Good, I actually danced." He nodded and then said, "Ok, now back to work."

The Wrong One

"Diane has seen you and would love to go out with you." I looked at Carol with what must have been a stunned expression. Carol laughed and said, "Really, I'm serious. I was right about where the Rose family lives. I bumped into Diane and her parents at the Shore Room last Tuesday night. We got talking and I mentioned you and how taken you were with her. I told her you worked with me and were a pretty cool guy. She laughed and said she might be interested. She would think about it. Well, she called me last night, told me she had seen you a few times from a distance and would love to go out. Here's her number." She handed me a piece of paper.

How often does a dream come true! That's what kept playing in my mind as I settled into my office chair reviewing applications for admission to Iona College. John Ng, who worked in the guidance department, had introduced me to Brother O'Toole, head of guidance, near the end of the first semester, and I had accepted a part-time job working in the office. It was a great move for me because Brother O'Toole took me under his wings and was a good mentor. Carol was Brother's secretary.

For over two months I had observed on and off this strikingly attractive college student walk past our house on Faneuil Street, turn right on Mayflower Avenue and head for the bus stop. Sometimes I observed her from our third floor apartment and on a few occasions, when the landlady wasn't home, I had seen her from the first floor. She had a satchel she carried on her left shoulder with the name College of New Rochelle on it. Once when I was walking up Mayflower, I saw her coming from the other direction and turn down Faneuil. I walked to the end of the block and in the distance I saw her enter a colonial house. I assumed she lived there.

Carol had grown up in New Rochelle and one day we happened to be chatting in the office. "Carol," I said, "I don't want you to think of me as a weirdo or stalker or something, but there is this girl — well, college student — I have seen a number of times walking by my house. I think she is a student at the College of New Rochelle, and couple of weeks ago I happened to be coming up Mayflower when she was coming down and then turned down Faneuil. I watched as she entered what I think is her home. Here is the address."

She took the piece of paper and looked at it. "Hummmm, this address sounds very familiar. I'm not sure, but it could be Tommy Rose's house — he's a good friend of my older brother. You know, I think I met Tommy's parents a couple of times at the Club. His father is a pretty good golfer and played with my Dad in a league if I remember correctly. And I do think Tommy has a younger sister. Mrs. Rose teaches at the high school." Carol looked at me and winked. "Let me see what I can find out. Who knows, Paul, if I'm right, you may meet your dream girl."

I slipped into Jim's room and slapped a little Chateau something on my face. He was alway bragging about how it brought the women running. I just wanted one woman running tonight. It was a bit on the cool side, so I wore a blazer over a sweater vest and a blue dress shirt. My plan was to walk to her house, then the two of us would walk to the bus stop, take the bus downtown, and then stroll to one of the coolest places in New Rochelle, the Barge, an old-fashioned, smoke-filled gin mill with a back deck that hung out over Long Island Sound. The buses ran until nearly midnight, so we would have plenty of time to get home.

"Diane will be right down," Ellen, her mom, said. A warm and gracious lady, she and I had immediately launched into a discussion of *Catcher in the Rye* when I saw it on her coffee table. "I was talking to the students today about the ice rink at Rockefeller and asked them, 'Isn't there always a Sally Hays?' One of them said, 'You mean someone who is so into themselves they see no one else?' I thought that was a good insight and said, 'Well yes, in a way — ah, here she is now.'"

The first section of stairs arrived at a landing and then the stairs turned a sharp right. Diane was on the landing, looked down at me, and just for a second — appeared puzzled, and then offered a warm and inviting smile.

"Hi, Paul," she said, "so good to meet you."

"Paul and I were just chatting about Holden," Ellen said, pointing to the book, "so nice to know that you have a well-read date. Well, have a great time. Anywhere special tonight?"

"I think we will just go down to the Barge for a while, maybe have a drink and a bite to eat," I said.

"The Barge, goodness, is that still floating?" Ellen said and then chuckled. "Listen, have a great night, you two."

We kind of filled each other in on our lives as we waited for and then rode the bus downtown. At the Barge, we sat at a table, had a beer, and split a burger. At one point, we walked out on the back deck which was very cool — the fog rolling in. I remember asking her if she had seen *A Streetcar Named Desire* with Brando, and she had. We agreed that the scene reminded us of that moment in the movie when Blanche tells her dark secret to Mitch on the deck of the Casino with the fog rolling in.

A short time after, we were dancing to "Smoke Gets in Your Eyes" — dancing was still a rare occurrence for me, but I loved the song — when I stopped moving and said to her, "I am not the Paul O'Brien you were thinking of, am I?" She smiled and said, "That's true." My mind had played that puzzled look over and over again on the bus and at the Barge — and then it had hit me. Across the street from me lived Paul V. O'Brien, a year ahead of me in college and also a boarder. When I thought further about it later, I remembered that as she walked down her street, his apartment was directly in line with her street, and she had probably seen him coming and going a number of times. I can't remember if I asked her how she had gotten to know of him, at least by name. But my question and her response kind of created a peacefulness in the scene. And we finished the dance.

We never went out again though we remained friends, and to my knowledge she never went out with Paul V. O'Brien.

The Historian

Freshman year in college was challenging for me, and money was tight. I worked in the Admissions Office and part-time at the food counter of a local drugstore. It was at the drugstore where I found my third job.

"Will that be all, Sir?" I asked as the tall gentleman was placing his napkin on the counter.

"Yes, Paul," he said. "That will about do it." He stood and reached for his wallet. "Let me ask you a question."

"Sure," I said.

"You said you're in your first year at the college, and you work here to make a few extra pennies. I could actually use some help with my work, only one morning a week, Saturdays. I live within walking distance of this place. It would just involve some typing and some organizing of papers, charts, etc. I could give you 50 dollars plus lunch. And so you don't have to keep calling me, 'Sir,' my name is William Dornfill."

"That's sounds pretty good, Mr. Dornfill — when would I start if I said yes?"

"Well, today is Tuesday, If you are able, you could start this Saturday. I will be back in Thursday night, and you can let me know then."

"Sounds good," I said, and I already knew my answer — that extra 50 bucks sounded great.

· · · · ·

I arrived at his place, a second floor flat on a street located about half way between my apartment and the drugstore where I worked. He had said that the work hours would be between 9:00 and 12:00 on Saturday morning. I arrived shortly before 9:00. He opened the door, and I entered a relatively small but busy flat. On the right side of the main work room was a desk with a portable typewriter on it, a number of accordion folders on the floor near the desk. To the left of the desk were two bookcases, both overflowing with well-worn books. He turned the chair at the desk and gestured for me to sit down. He then sat down in an easy chair.

"Paul, a lot of my work involves corresponding with Civil War historians and coordinating material for the Library of Congress. I have developed over the years, as you may have noticed" — he held up his hands — "some pretty severe arthritis in my hands, and one of the effects is that typing is very painful for me. You can be a great help with my correspondence if you can do the typing — basically I will dictate what you will type."

"I think I can do that," I said.

"Wonderful," he said, "let's begin — and remember we stop at noon, and it's lunch on me."

And so we begin, my work involved taking down his dictation, proofreading once when I was done, and then handing the typed page to him for a final look. If he found a mistake or two, that meant that I would type it one more time. I didn't realize at the time the stature of the men I was typing the letters to: Bruce Catton, Shelby Foote, Allan Nevins, and Paul Buck — a few of the names I remember probably because over time these four seemed to pop up a lot in history classes, and then I actually read some of their work. There was some filing I had to do, connected with mail he had received and sometimes he would let that go for a few days. And at the end of the work session, before we went out to lunch, we had one ritual, strange, but I got used to it — we would Indian wrestle.

He would lie down on the floor, and I would lie down next to him, my head next to his feet, and vice versa. On the count of one, each of us would lift the leg next to each other up to a vertical position, then legs back down, on the count of two, same thing, and on the count of three, the legs would go up and interlock and each of us would try to win by bringing the other's leg down, as in arm-wrestling. The first time we did it, I felt it was pretty strange, but it became a regular thing, even though I don't think I ever won. He was much taller than I and had longer legs.

I worked almost every Saturday, and he always paid me right before we left for lunch, at a variety of diners and restaurants in the New Rochelle area. Of course, I was never allowed to pay for lunch. Once when I was admiring his white Chevy convertible parked outside the restaurant, he said, "You are welcome to use my car if you ever need one." I looked up at him, "Wow, Mr. D. that's really nice of you."

"Sure," he said. "Got any big dances coming up?"

As a matter of fact I did. The girl I was dating had invited me to Manhattanville's Freshmen Dance in late April. "Maybe," I said, thinking I might wait on the specific request, "that's awfully nice of you."

· · · · ·

Sometime in early March, he told me that on the following weekend he had to drive up to the Catskills to look at the printing press that his publisher used, and he would love to have company. "We could take a leisurely drive up Saturday morning, stop for lunch some place, and when we reach the facility, take a look at the press and then stay over at the house that is part of the complex and drive back on Sunday. I'll bring some food for dinner and breakfast."

I think I was still hoping to borrow his Chevy for the dance, so I thought that I should stay in his especially good graces. "I think I can do that," I said. "I'll just throw a few things in my duffle bag, and be ready to go on Saturday."

The little compound — a few buildings, one of which held the printing press — was at the end of a long back road that meandered through a lot of woods. After he showed me my room at the top of the stairs, with a bathroom across the hall, he said, "I'll give you a tour." The first room we entered off the hallway downstairs was a library with wall-to-wall books. "Wow," I said, "this is impressive."

"Feel free to browse. If you see something you like, grab it. And you don't have to worry about getting it back quickly — I know where you live." He laughed. "Do you know this one?" he asked, pulling a book from the shelf near him — "*Lady Chatterly's Lover* by D. H. Lawrence — it's a good one. You might want to check it out." He set it down on a table in front of the books. There was a small dining room off the kitchen, with only three chairs and an old oak table, and in the room next to that an ancient sofa and one easy chair, facing an ancient television.

A bit later, he gave me a tour of the building that held the print operation. "During the week, there are three men who work here," he said, "kind of an old fashioned operation, but they are good at it, from typesetter to the actual printer."

It seemed kind of primitive to me, but the machines glistened and looked as if they were ready to roll.

For dinner that night, we had fried chicken and baked potatoes. "You told me you love potatoes, so I had to have them as part of the meal," he said. I thanked him, joked about how crucial potatoes were in Irish families, and then we chatted a bit about his upcoming projects. After dinner, we had some decaffeinated coffee and, to my delight, he offered me a slice of apple pie, with a scoop of vanilla ice cream. "Pretty nice," I said. We talked a bit longer, and then I stretched and said, "Well, I think I'll head up and start to think about retiring. It's been a long day, but a good one."

"Agreed," he said. "It has been a long day. Breakfast will be at 8:00 sharp. Do you need a wakeup call so you can have a shower first?"

"No thanks, I have my trusty alarm," I said. "See you at 8:00 for breakfast."

. . . . .

I was restless in the night and felt a bit uneasy about the morning, so I decided I would play things safely. The bathroom was right across the landing from my room. I went into the bathroom, stripped down to only my shorts, and then turned the shower on. I reached in and with my right hand threw some water on myself, and then I stopped the shower. I could hear him coming up the stairs. I grabbed the towel and put it in front of me with the drops of water still visible on my shoulder and face.

I opened the door, and Mr. Dornfill was standing right there, "Oh," he said, "done already?"

"I always take really quick showers," I said. "My roommate from China taught me that."

He stared at me. It was very awkward, and then I said, "I will be down in just in few."

"Sure," he said, turning, and then he walked slowly down the stairs.

I felt that I had dodged something, but I wasn't exactly sure what.

. . . . .

On the following Saturday, I went to his house, but there was no answer. I walked downstairs and knocked on the owner's door. I had met Mrs. Jones a few times, coming and going, and she seemed like a good soul. She opened her door, "Hi, Paul. Sorry about your friend going so fast."

"What happened?"

"On Tuesday, he came down and told me that for a number of reasons — he couldn't go into them — he had to pack up and leave. The moving van was coming the following day, and he was really apologetic and said that he wouldn't accept no to the fact that he was going to pay an additional two months rent because of his very sudden departure. I tried to argue that that was not necessary, but he insisted. On Wednesday late in the afternoon, he came in to thank me for letting him rent what was for him a perfect apartment. And then he said good bye and gave me a little hug."

"Wow, he didn't leave any notes or anything?"

"Nothing. The place was immaculate when I went up to look."

"Do you know where he went?" I asked.

"He never gave me a forwarding address — probably worked that out with the post office."

"Yeah, I guess so. Well, thank you, Mrs. Jones. Take care of yourself."

"Bye, Paul. Glad we got to know each other a bit."

And that was the story of Mr. Dornfill, one of those people who enter your life for a while, leave their imprint, and then disappear. Forever.

· · · · ·

But not quite. Years later, Debbie and I were chatting with a close friend who had grown up in New Rochelle. I happened to refer to the historian and mentioned the street that he lived on. Kevin knew the street and said, "Let me check." He Googled the name and found a number of articles and his obituary. He had spent his life primarily as a Civil War historian, had remained single, and for a period of a few years had lived in New Rochelle. The obituary said that he died at his small home in the Catskills in 1990.

When I think about Mr. Dornfill today, my guess is that he was gay and quite repressed. The early 60's was still a period, as I recall, when being gay was not accepted by most. I wonder now if he struggled with intentions he might have had toward me, and if the trip to the Catskills had given him some thought and maybe hope about a relationship beyond the friendship. I also wonder if what appeared to be his precipitous departure from New Rochelle was connected to our trip to the Catskills and expectations that were not met.

Dangerous Water

For me, it was usually scrambled eggs, home fries, and wheat toast, with coffee of course. At first I was the subject of some mockery, "Eggs are for breakfast, O'Brien." But then it wasn't long before Bill and Tony started ordering eggs too. Mike was the exception tonight, going for the BLT. Of course, it didn't matter that it was often 11:00 at night at the diner, when a few of us felt hungry and decided that we needed a break from the books. The short order cook on the grill was ready and willing to serve up whatever we wanted. Actually the College Diner was probably the most popular spot on North Avenue for Iona students. I mean it was there waiting for us with open arms as we walked out the main entrance of the college.

The thing about diners is that you can really be yourself, laugh a little louder, tease a little more. On this particular evening there were four of us in a booth having a good time, when Bill looked up from his plate, "What the hell is going on?" He stood up next to the booth, "God, it's Jimmy." We were up instantly, and I turned toward the main door — it fed into a small outer waiting room with an exterior door. At the outer door was Jimmy, a member of our class and an outstanding cross country runner, now on his knees — his hands pressing on the window of the door. Blood ran down his face — behind him were three guys who were punching him and kicking him, shouting, "Take that, college fucking asshole." We tried to rush the interior door to get to Jimmy, but it was blocked by the owner, a big bruiser of a dude, — "NO, this is not going to turn into a major brawl."

"God damn," Bill yelled, "he is getting pounded to shit out there." You could see them punching Jimmy in the head, and then stepping back and kicking him. "Come on," Bill screamed — " they'll kill him."

The owner must have heard the word "kill" and maybe didn't want a murder on his property. He held his hand up — the whole restaurant was now standing and looking — as if to stop the wave. "Nobody move," he shouted.

He yanked the interior door open, stepping into the waiting room, and with sheer force, pushed the outer door open, with Jimmy up against it and his three assailants still attacking. "Get the fuck out of here, you creeps," he screamed and then he reached out and pretty much dragged Jimmy in as the three attackers backed up and then took off down North Avenue.

I remember the diner sacrificing a few dish towels to clean Jimmy up, who to our amazement wasn't as injured as badly as we thought — a few head wounds and bruises but nothing apparently gaping or major. If anything, he was dealing with his own shock at the incident. "I was just walking by the Tower on my way when this gang of guys started saying stuff like 'Asshole,' and 'Who let you out tonight?' I just looked at them — same crowd as always hangs out there — and walked on, when I heard someone say, 'Let's get this fuckface.' And then they were after me. I would've outrun them, but I tripped on a rut in the sidewalk, and by the time I reached here, they'd caught me."

The police arrived and Jimmy's roommate showed up — he had a car. After the police took down the report, Dave, the roomie, said, "Jimmy says he's ok, but I am going to take him down to the emergency room — some of those cuts may need a few stitches."

Thinking about it now, I remember feeling totally helpless, as if I were going to pass out, especially that minute or two when they kept beating Jimmy, and we were blocked from helping him. It seemed so brutal.

Outside, Tony said, "Listen, I know who the guys are that Jimmy's talking about — one of them was outside the Tower tonight when we walked by — bunch of deadbeats. You know I think we should give them a lesson."

"I'm in," Mike said, "We don't have to take that shit from these losers."

"My car is ready to roll, " Bill said, "We just have to get us some needed equipment."

I remember thinking that this was not a wise idea, but, unlike Trey years later in *Boyz n the Hood,* I did not get out of the car. Mike had his bat, Tony didn't need anything because he had a belt in karate. I had a belt with a huge buckle that Bill had let me take for the occasion, and Bill had a pair of gloves with some type of brass attachment. We drove up and down Mayflower and then cruised down to Main Street, but we did not see anyone. "They're gone," Bill said, laughing. "They heard we were out to take a little vengeance. And they are scared shitless. So gentlemen, I guess we head for home, give Dave a ring to see how Jimmy is, and call it a night."

In the back seat, I breathed a sigh of relief. I had never done anything like this in my life, and frankly, I was terrified inside, and I don't think I would have had the courage to swing that belt at anyone. Walking to my apartment, I felt a tremendous sense of relief, relief that we had not met the gang members and "settled things." No question as I look back on that night, we had entered dangerous waters.

Danielle

On that warm afternoon, the gazpacho was perfect. I had ordered a bowl and an iced tea and was settling in with my New York dailies: the *News* and the *Post*. Ambition, a local downtown eating establishment, was still sprinkled with a few customers, and I could see the owner busy in the small kitchen off the bar. I had noticed when I first sat down a drape across a section of the back room — sort of a lounge area — and was a bit curious about what the drape concealed. As I took another spoon of the soup, I heard the drape slide part way open, and a woman emerged, maybe in her mid-forties, wearing a bright yellow-flowered dress.

"Excuse me," I said, as she neared my booth, "but could I ask you what is going on back there."

"Oh, sure," she said, "there's a palm reader who tells you about your life."

"Ah, is she good?"

"Actually, very good. She was definitely worth it."

"What's her fee?" I asked.

"Twenty dollars for thirty minutes — you should try it. Her name and her fee are on that card standing up at the end of the bar."

"Thank you," I said. As she strolled out, I turned the page of the *Post* and continued to eat my soup, but I kept thinking about the mysterious woman behind the curtain who according to the departing lady, "was definitely worth it."

After I had paid the bill, I noticed the owner standing near the end of the bar. I walked over and said, "Very good gazpacho." He nodded and said, "Thanks." I glanced at the card advertising the woman behind the drape — "Danielle, Your Reading."

"I heard she's good," I said, pointing at the card.

"Everybody I've talked to who went in today indicated that she was good," he said, "maybe seven people so far."

"You know what," I said, "I'm going to give her a whirl."

"Good for you," he said. "You pay her at the end."

· · · · ·

She sat at a small table, a chair across from her for her client. Dressed in dark pants and a purple blouse, she looked up, gave a warm smile, and said, "Welcome and your first name — that's all I want to know — is?"

"Paul," I said, as I took a seat.

"Thank you, Paul. We will spend a little time together, and I will offer you some thoughts based on what I read in you. To start, I will need your right hand."

"Sure," I said, offering my hand.

"Have you had readings before?" she asked.

"No" — the dark table felt very smooth — "but I am intrigued since people are saying you are quite good."

"Well, I will speak the truth I feel in my heart, Paul."

I didn't know this world of palm reading or fortune-telling, and I had no idea whether her approach was standard or atypical, but I do remember that she began by running her fingertips from the left side of my hand up the pinky finger and back down; then up and down each of the three remaining fingers, and then after coming down the index finger, she circled up and over the thumb and back down along the base of the palm and then rested her four fingers in the center of my palm, her thumb sliding under to rest gently against the back of my hand. She focused on her fingers in my hand.

"Paul, I feel a strength in the center, in the core, perhaps a strong moral force that runs through you. I am associating that with a person, Paul, who has been strength for you and a powerful influence."

I nodded and muttered something like, "Um-mmmmmm."

"Paul, I am feeling the letter A as the first letter of this person's name."

I did all my best to remain calm and neutral because I wanted to see if there was anything to this stuff, but the letter A had a ring to it for me — the strongest influence in my childhood and continuing to inform my thinking as an adult was my mother, whose name was Anna. I said nothing.

"I sense a strong bond in your family, a closeness that finds its source in this person whose name starts with the letter A. She lifted her fingers up gently and then began to trace the lines in my hand — I had heard that the lines represented things like fate, life-line, health, but it was all vague to me. And I was starting to feel almost the way you feel after a drink or two — perhaps it was also her touch on my hand.

"Paul, you have an empathetic nature. I can tell that you work with people, possibly as a teacher or maybe some type of social worker, but people matter." Her fingers were now moving very slowly over the lines of my hand.

"And, Paul, though you are good with people, you must have time to reflect — my sense is that you find sources of strength in certain people, but also in reading and quiet time alone. Without this source of strength and nourishment, you would feel empty."

I remember there were other connections that rang true that session, not all, but enough to make me believe that this woman had gifts as a seer — at least for me. At the end, she stressed the need to maintain balance in my life — continue to be present to others but as important take time to think and read and reflect. Her dark brown eyes looked right at me. "Keep bringing peace," she said.

She had connected with my mother, my career of teaching high school English, the vital place of talking with others, the need for reading, and the importance of solitude.

"Danielle, thank you," I said, after paying her the twenty dollars. "All I can say is that I feel a kind of peace, that someone else has an understanding of me."

"Paul," she had a warm smile, "it's been a pleasure to sit with you for this short period. I wish you well as you continue your journey."

I remember leaving Ambition feeling buoyant and connected, and I felt that it was definitely worth the twenty dollars.

· · · · ·

Time passed — I think two years. During that time, I did one thing I had been avoiding for a few years — I joined Facebook, after some cajoling by Tina, a graduate of the high school where I taught. "You will love it, reconnect to so many students you taught, and, so you don't have to fret, it's your call whether you want to accept friends or not." And so, I did, unlike a number of teacher friends who stayed away from the dreaded Facebook. One night, I turned Facebook on and there on what I call the home page was a posting for Danielle's Palm Reading. I read the brief description and noted the phone number. Things had been happening in my life and decisions were on the horizon, and I thought, "Danielle, yes, it's time to chat again."

We were to meet in the lobby of the Parker Inn in downtown Schenectady on a Tuesday afternoon at 3:00. I was there at 2:45 or so and stood outside the Inn watching people scurry to and fro. At 3:00, I walked inside, looked around, and then ambled through the bar area and out into Proctor's Arcade where I looked from one end to the other — no sign of Danielle. I waited there for a few minutes; then I walked out to State Street and gazed up and down — lots of people but no Danielle. I walked to the front of the Parker Inn again and stood there. Glancing at my watch — it was now 3:20 — I thought, "Well, something must have happened or she forgot. Time to go."

I was just passing Gershon's on Upper Union Street when my phone rang. I pulled into an open spot in front of Trustco, a local bank. "Hello," I said. "Paul, this is Danielle. Where are you? I have been waiting for almost a half hour." Something had gone wrong. "I was there, Danielle. I looked all over for you — inside the Parker Inn and in the Arcade. Out on the Street. I didn't see you. I left about 15 minutes ago."

"Parker Inn?" she said.

"Yes, that's where we agreed to meet."

"No, no," she said. "I told you the Hampton Inn downtown."

I was pretty sure it was the Parker Inn, but I decided to not argue. "Well, I am sorry for the confusion. Maybe another time."

"Paul, I still have time today for you."

"Really," — I glanced at my watch, almost 3:45, but I didn't have anywhere crucial to be. "I can turn around and be down to the Hampton Inn in about 10."

"That's great," she said. "See you shortly."

. . . . .

As I was getting out of my car, which I had parked across the street from the Hampton, I noticed a tall, casually dressed man talking in what seemed to be a serious vein to Danielle and another woman, somewhat shorter than Danielle and quite stocky. I paused for a second and then the man stepped back, turned, and went on up the street.

"Hi," I said to Danielle, who said, "Hi" back and then turned to the other woman, "Linda, this is Paul, you know, the nice man I told you about whose palm I read some time ago." Linda offered her hand, and I shook it, "Nice to meet you," I said.

Danielle was already moving toward the entranceway, and Linda and I followed. Once inside, Danielle headed toward a somewhat separate room off the main lounge. You could see the busy street outside, "I hope it's ok that we meet in here," I said to Linda as we walked. "It's ok," she said, "Danielle talked to the person at the desk."

Danielle sat down in a chair, and I moved another chair to a few feet in front of her. Linda sat down to my right, only a few feet away. I thought it was strange that Linda was now going to be in on Danielle's reading of me, but I turned and focused. I held out my right hand and Linda touched it with both of hers — there was a tension in her that I had not felt before.

"Let me see if I can get of sense of where you are now," she said, and I felt the irony. "Now her right hand was gently touching my right hand, and she started to trace lines that she could see but not smoothly. When I glanced up at her, I saw her eyes filling and then tears. "I'm sorry," she said.

"Danielle has had a bad week," Linda said. "She had to leave her boyfriend's house up in Luzerne and take care of herself." Linda reached over and touched Danielle's shoulder. Danielle was now blowing her nose. "Paul, Danielle is at the Women's Shelter now, and when she goes out, someone has to go with her. We were actually escorted down here. She said she wanted to meet with you today, and I said I would accompany her. Danielle, do you want to say anything?"

"I'm so sorry — this is supposed to be about you." Her hands were back on the table and I touched her right hand gently. "Don't worry about me today," I said.

"Thank you, Paul." She looked out at the street and then she breathed deeply and looked at me, "Well, it's not good — my boyfriend has a bad temper, and when he has a few drinks, he can do anything." As she was talking, I noticed dark marks on her neck that I hadn't noticed before. "Last week," — she glanced over at Linda who nodded, 'It's ok,' — "I don't even know what I did. It was about 8:00, just getting dark, and he was angry about something. I tried to tell him how he should handle a landscaping situation, and he began screaming at me ... 'Fucking bitch, shut the fuck up.' I still tried to say something, and he charged at me, grabbing me by the hair, and shoving me out into the hallway. 'You should take a little ride, you fucking bitch.' And then he threw me down the stairs." Her whole body was shaking, and Linda got up and walked next to Danielle and put her arms around her.

"It's ok, you don't have to go on," I said.

Danielle looked at me and continued, her body shaking, "At the bottom of the stairs, I heard my next door neighbor — older gentleman always going for walks — knocking at the door, 'All right in there? Danielle?' Then Tony came down the stairs — 'Getting the whole fucking world involved, D?' "He grabbed the door and ripped it open."

"Everybody ok in there?" my neighbor asked.

"Yeah, fuckface, none of your fucking business."

"I think John, my neighbor, saw my foot extended out on the floor. 'Danielle,' he said, 'You ok.'"

"I told you to get the fuck out of here," Tony said, "and then he punched John. I heard John scream out, 'Jeeeessssuuuuuuusssss!' And then I heard John say, 'I think you broke my nose! I'm calling the cops right now!'"

"Tony slammed the door shut, but he didn't see that I had grabbed a piece of kindling wood from the pile leaning against the wall. The piece I had grabbed had a jagged end, and as Tony was about to punch me again — 'You're getting more, Bitch,' I thrust the wood as hard as I could and felt it rip into his side, below the rib cage."

"'Cocksucker!' he screamed and fell backward on the stairs."

Her body was still shaking, and she was crying, "I am not sure how I did it, but I got up, yanked the door open, and took off, disappearing into the woods." She stopped and looked at Linda. "I mean, it was not that bad. I know the woods well, and I knew the way to a friend's house. As I made my way along an old path, I could hear a siren drawing closer to our place."

Danielle squeezed Linda's arm, "And my friend, Maggie, got me to the women's shelter, where I feel kind of safe and I have people like Linda to help me out."

I reached out with my two hands and touched her right hand. "Oh my God. What a terrible thing to happen to you. It's a nightmare. Thank God, you're safe now."

"I remembered somehow that I had made this appointment with you and didn't want to miss it," she said.

Linda stepped back and took her seat.

"Jesus," I said. "You have a lot bigger issues to deal with than I do. You need to do all that you can to get your life back together."

Danielle nodded, rubbing her eyes with a tissue, and then Linda said, "Well, for now she is safe, and we are trying to do all the basic things we can — find her a longer-term place to stay where she is safe for a starter."

"Listen," I said, "I won't keep you any longer." I had slid my wallet out of my front left pocket and had retrieved a twenty and a ten. I folded them up, and then I reached out and said, "Take this, and I hope you can find a place and some peace."

"No, I can't," Danielle said. "I didn't do anything for you today. I should be paying you."

"Danielle, you shared your story with me. That's enough."

I stood up and reached out to shake Linda's hand, "Thank you," and then I stepped around the table and gave Danielle a small hug. "Oh my God, I wish you the best," I said.

As I was exiting the Inn, I had another thought. I paused and jotted down on a piece of paper my phone number. I stepped back in and met them by the door. I gave Linda the folded piece of paper and said, "If there is anything I can do, call me." She looked at me and said, "Thank you."

· · · · ·

About a week later, I got a call one morning from Linda. "Hi, Paul. Big request. Is it possible to meet Danielle downtown this afternoon — I can't be there but Abby, another shelter volunteer, will be with Danielle."

"I can probably do that," I said.

73

"Great. Where to meet …. I'm not sure that the Inn is a good spot."

"How about Ambition on Jay Street?"

"That sounds good," she said.

"Ahhhh, maybe 2:00?"

"Perfect, I will tell Abby, and the two of them will see you at 2:00 at Ambition.

· · · · ·

When I arrived a little before two, they were already seated with their backs to the door in one of the booths that runs along the right side of the wall. I slid into the seat across from them, with Danielle closer to the wall. I held out my hand, "Hi, Abby, I'm Paul." She took my hand, while saying, "Nice to meet you," gave it a couple of shakes and let go. "Hi, Danielle, " I said, and she responded with a soft "Hi" and a nod.

"Can I get you guys something to drink and would you like to see a menu," a somewhat disheveled waiter asked.

"I'll have an iced tea with lemon," I said. "You guys?"

"Diet Coke for me," Abby said, and Danielle nodded with a soft "Me too." As I looked at her in the corner, she seemed to have shrunken, like a creature trying to disappear.

We talked a bit about a couple of posters on the wall, and then the waiter arrived with our drinks. "You guys want any food?" They both shook their heads no, and I said to the waiter, "This will be it. Thanks."

Abby leaned forward and said, "We're doing ok at the shelter, but a complication has developed. Danielle's boyfriend has been calling her on her cell. She won't answer, but we are afraid that he is going to figure out where she is, maybe trace the phone or something. So we need to take some action, and we were wondering if you could help."

Danielle sat up a bit in the booth. "If I can," I said.

"Danielle, uh, here's the issue — if Danielle had a new phone with a new number, she would be free of his attempts to reach her. The other good thing we are trying to do is to get her into another shelter, maybe in Albany, but right now there is no room."

"How much would a new phone cost" I said.

"We have done some checking — we can get her one for about 60 dollars, you know a fairly decent phone."

I looked at Danielle, and she looked back and then down, almost, I felt, embarrassed that Abby was making this request.

"I could probably do that," I said. "When could you get the phone?"

"We can do it this afternoon," Abby said.

"Ok," I said. I had been to the bank that morning and had about a hundred dollars in cash. I took out three twenties and handed them to Abby.

"Thanks, Paul," she said, "this is a huge help." Danielle gave a little smile and whispered, "Thank you."

When we exited, I headed left towards my parked car, and they went right, in the direction of the shelter that they had come from. As I walked, I thought of how much Danielle had changed from a confident palm reader dispensing helpful advice to a weak and almost helpless person. I hoped my sixty dollars would be put to the right use.

. . . . .

I was in the car weeks later with my nephew who was visiting from Virginia. We were heading to see *The Matrix* when my cell phone rang. I slowed down and pulled to the side of the road.

"Hello," I could barely hear her voice, but I knew.

"Danielle, what's going on?"

"I'm on the street in downtown Schenectady outside the Proctor's Arcade."

Justin was staring ahead. "Ok, any plans from there?" I asked.

"I got thrown out," she said.

"Of the shelter?"

"Yes, and there is nowhere for me to go," she was now crying.

I wasn't sure what Justin was making of this conversation, but I felt I had to take a strong step at this point. "Danielle, there is nothing I can do."

"I have nowhere to go, " she said. "You are the only one I can reach out to."

My mind was reeling, and my Catholic guilt was rising. Then I remembered someone, "Danielle, listen to me. Here's what you need to do. Go up the street to St. Joseph's Church and go to the rectory. Right up the street about two blocks. Ask for Father Hogan. Tell him your story. He will be able to help you."

All I could hear was her sobbing. "Danielle, I've got to go. Please do that. Go to St. Joseph's and ask for Father Hogan. I have to go, Danielle."

And then I closed my phone. I looked at Justin and said, "A friend who is in trouble, but I don't think I can do anymore for her. Father Hogan is a good man who has found refuge for street people before. If anyone can help her, he can."

Justin looked ahead and nodded, and then we drove on.

· · · · ·

Months later, on a Sunday afternoon, Debbie and I attended Mass at St. Joseph's, not our normal routine, but we had been out late on Saturday night and decided to skip morning Mass. Even though my mind was drifting off to different projects I had due for the coming week, Father Hogan's deep baritone voice kept pulling me back. And the reading that he was reflecting on was the Parable of the Good Samaritan. What does it mean, he asked, to reach out to someone in need, and how far will we go to see that our neighbor's needs are met. For the Good Samaritan dressed the man's wounds, took him to an inn where he could rest and heal, and then payed the innkeeper to care for the man. How far will we go to be a neighbor? To be like Christ?

Father Hogan stood in the back shaking hands with people as they exited the Church. Part of me wanted to wait and quietly ask him if a woman named Danielle had come to see him a few months ago and if he had been able to do anything for her. Instead, when I reached him, I simply said, "Thank you, Father."

Lost and Found

I stood facing Debbie who was sitting up on the edge of the sofa in a lounge area outside Apple Computer. "Nope," I said. "Nothing." And at that moment my eyes filled, and I knew I was on the edge of losing it. "Someone picked it up," I said. "It's gone."

The week leading up to this moment had gone well, for the most part. And for me, it had been a pretty significant week. With much encouragement from my wife and my niece and her family in the Mid-West, I had decided to visit my niece in Bloomington, Illinois. Carolyn is one of my favorite people in the world. She is a warm and welcoming person, and a person of some accomplishment. An author of a number of books and a professor of Spanish at Illinois Wesleyan University, she and her husband Chad have raised four children while overcoming some serious physical illnesses along the journey. So, though I don't like flying, being with Carolyn and her family was a strong incentive, and my trip was made easier in that Carolyn was going to be in Chicago the day I arrived, having driven up for a Conference. Instead of having to transfer to another flight south to Bloomington, I would ride down with Carolyn, about a two hour drive, after the conference. Perfect.

Carolyn and Chad's house is an Upstairs-Downstairs, Post-Victorian built in the early twentieth century. At the time I arrived, two of their four children were still living at home: Daniel and Ethan. Miranda was working in Australia, and Camille was a sophomore at Bradley University in Illinois. Carolyn put me in Camille's room on the second floor. What made this location unique for me was that the second floor landing had two sets of stairs, one on the left and one on the right that descended to the first floor. Depending on which stairs I ascended, the direction at the top was the opposite from what I would have taken if I had ascended the other set of stairs. Stairs became a key motif.

My three full days with Carolyn and Chad were wonderful. Carolyn lives only a few blocks from Illinois Wesleyan University, so on a lovely spring Saturday, after a hearty breakfast prepared by Chad, she and I walked to the campus and she gave me a tour. On one of the walls of the building that included Carolyn's office and classroom was a quotation from a former IWU President, Minor Myers: "Go into the world and do well. But more importantly, go into the world and do good." It was exciting to stand in the room and see where Carolyn, as a friend of mine describes the work of teaching, "plies her craft." It was also very cool when shortly after we met a prospective student with her Mom on the steps of the library. Carolyn talked easily with the student, as she did a short time after with some of the softball players who were coming off the field after the end of the first game of a double header.

Carolyn had some work at the University on Monday, and Chad and I set out to visit Camille at Bradley University. As I recall it seemed about a 45 minute drive or so, and it was enlightening to listen to Chad talk about the land, the wind-powered energy — giant wind mills prevalent on the flat land, and the struggle of the farmers to make a living. We picked up Camille near her dorm, drove around town a

bit, and then headed to one of Chad's favorite diners out-
side town. Camille, a bright young woman, was a sociology
major who had become active in student government and
was excited about the prospects of what could be done to
improve campus life.

The Burger Barge was a ram-shackled sprawling affair
totally without pretensions and dedicated to giving the cus-
tomer what they wanted. It was one of Chad's favorites,
and I knew the food would be good. I think Chad and I
each had a beer, and I recall that I got a burger (What
choice really — I mean a barge loaded with burgers), fries,
and a side salad. We had some laughs, talked about college
life, and the politics of the world. It was a good setting, per-
fect for a relaxed and enjoyable chat.

After lunch we dropped Camille off at college and
headed back to Bloomington. Gazing out the window at
the towering windmills, I thought of the high point of a
fund-raiser we had put on at my high school in memory or
a beloved teacher and director of musicals. At one moment,
one of the graduates who had played Sancho Panza in our
school production of *Man of La Mancha* came out to sing
"The Impossible Dream," accompanied by his brother. Be-
fore beginning, he announced that the song was in memory
of another student who had played Don Quixote in the
play. The other student had died the year before of drug
complications. Behind the two singers was a windmill, the
perfect symbol for the world of Don Quixote and the song.

After a good nap, I drifted down to the kitchen, kind
of the headquarters and starting point for all action in the
household. My niece announced that we were going to one
of their favorite Italian restaurants in town. Sounded great
to me, and shortly after, Carolyn, Chad, their son Daniel,
and I were off to Lucca's Grill. In this cozy place, we sat at

a table near the bar and feasted on salad and two pizzas: A spicy veggie and a cheese. I remember Daniel talking in a spirited way about his plans to major in film study at De-Paul, which he would attend in the fall.

Back at the house, we pulled into the garage about 8 p.m. In the car, we had been talking about the circular racing their dog had done in the back yard in the afternoon, and I said, "I know there is a word for that. My sister-in-law would know." I texted her just before I got out of the back of the car. I started to walk when I saw her answer, "Zoomies," and then I was falling head first into darkness. I struck something hard, and I looked back up at my feet resting on cement steps. In addition to the steps leading up to the kitchen, there were steps leading down to the root cellar. I did not see the root cellar steps. I remember seeing Chad's face appear near my feet and then Carolyn's. "Oh dear," she said, "are you ok?" All I knew was the truth of the line, "I've fallen and I can't get up." I think I said, "I need help," and each of them reached down to grab my arms extended upwards.

I remember my head stinging and pressing my right hand on top of my head. "I didn't see the steps," I said. "But are you ok?" Carolyn asked, and I took my hand off my head and saw that it was covered in blood. "Oh dear, I think we've got to get you to the hospital. We'll go the emergency room at St. Joe's — it's a good hospital, I had three kids there."

We arrived at the emergency room in twenty minutes or so, and saw that it was a pretty busy night — not horrific stuff, but plenty of people looking depressed and in pain. I think that I was given a clean cloth for my head, but we had to remain in the central waiting room for at least an hour or so before I was given a room where I could be examined. Carolyn and Chad were there with me as the nurse looked at my head and saw the wound. She said that the next procedure would be a Cat-Scan. I was wheeled to a room where the procedure was done and then back to the room I had been given. The nurse said it would be a while before the doctor would be there. Carolyn looked over at Chad who appeared exhausted and then back at me, "I'm going to run Chad home, and then I will come back to be here with you."

At a few points during the evening, I had texted Debbie and filled her in on what was going on. I also communicated with my brother who is a physician in Boston. Both were concerned but reassuring. I do remember during the evening that at a number of moments, I had looked up at the Crucifix on the wall and thought how encouraging that was. Carolyn returned and said that she had texted her siblings about what had happened, and one of them had said, "What are you trying to do? Kill one of our favorite uncles?"

We had arrived about 8:30 or so and it was closing in on 4:00 in the morning when the doctor entered the room to treat my head. Carolyn must have known what staples in the head feel like because she sat down next to me and said, "Better hold my hand." I have seen staples go into wood and heard the sound the gun makes when it shoots a sta-ple out. Now my head was the target, and the stapling had begun — no question — it hurt, and I squeezed Carolyn's hand hard. After the sixth staple, the doctor said, "Just two more" — "Thunk!" and finally "Thunk!" And it was over.

I think we got home about 5:30 in the morning, and I went up to my room and slipped into a sort of seated posi-tion on the bed and drifted off to sleep. About 7:30 Carolyn woke me. She was heading off to the University and wanted to say good-bye. We both laughed at how great a trip it had been until the last night, and then we both laughed at that. I told her I promised I would return some day, and this time I wanted a tour of the root cellar. In a little while Chad would drive me up to Chicago so that I could catch an early afternoon plane back to Albany.

On the way home, I looked again at my cell phone that had flown out of my hands as I was falling down the stairs. There was a diagonal crack across the front and though Chad said he thought it was just on the protective glass, I figured I would check it out at my local AT&T.

When I did, I was told that I would need a new glass cover, and that it was cheaper if I took it to Apple than if they did it. Two days later Debbie and I traveled down to Crossgates Mall and shortly after I stood outside the Apple store saying the word "Nothing."

While I was waiting for my cell phone to be repaired, I decided to try the massage chair. For five dollars, a person can have a 15 minute massage. The massage felt good, and after I went back to sit in the lounge area outside Apple where Debbie was waiting. We had been chatting for about five minutes when I moved in the chair and realized something was missing — I reached for my pocket and felt the absence of my wallet. "Oh my God," I said, "my wallet. I will be right back." I knew before I got to the massage chairs that I would find nothing. And I didn't. In my wallet, I had over two hundred dollars in cash that was obvious, and then tucked away were two hundred dollar bills. And of course, there were my five credit cards. I stood in front of Debbie, feeling the pain from the staples and now realizing that I had just lost my wallet — I was ready to cry. When she said, "You need to ask the security guard if he picked it up or saw anyone. The same guard has walked by four or five times since I have been here. There he is."

I had noticed him myself at one point — a husky, handsome, dark-haired guy maybe in his early thirties — and I quickly approached him, "Excuse me, I have a quick question for you."

"Sure," he said.

"By any chance, did you see a wallet near the massage chairs?"

"Yes, I did," he said "and I turned it in."

"Really? Well I lost mine sometime in the last 30 minutes."

"Hold on, let me call the office. What is your name?"

"Paul O'Brien."

"Heh," he said to someone in the office, "this is Nasir. The wallet I turned in twenty minutes ago. Can you check the name in it?" He looked at me while waiting, "Yes, uh huh. Good and thanks. He will be right up." He clicked the phone off and said, "Yes, it's yours. The office is on the third floor. It's there for you."

"That's incredible," I said and, "Thank you so much."

"Just doing my job," he said. "I always turn in things I find."

I looked back at Debbie and signaled a thumbs-up and then gestured that I would be back in a few. Still amazed that the wallet had been turned in, I knew in my heart that it would not have the over $400 dollars in it and that my credit cards would be missing. A few years prior, I had lost my wallet at Stewart's — I had paid for something there and then gotten to my destination and noticed that I did not have my wallet. I concluded that as I got into the car, balancing my coffee and hard roll, that the wallet had probably slipped out of my right pocket and fallen to the parking lot. When I got back to Stewart's there was no sign of a wallet. About ten months later on a Sunday afternoon, the doorbell rang. I was snoozing and Debbie was out, so I ignored it. About an hour later, I got up and went to the door to check to see if some political flyer was attached to the knob. Instead there was a plastic bag and in it was my wallet, well-seasoned for almost a year outside. The note said, "I am a surveyor in Niskayuna and found your wallet along River Road. Here are the coordinates"; and he had left me the coordinates of the exact location. The only thing of significance still left in the wallet was my license, a few meaningless cards, and some movie passes given to me by my friend Tom Maguire — at that point, they were beyond use.

I entered the security office. Four or five people in blue stood behind the counter. "Can I help you?" one asked.

"Yes, I lost my wallet and just spoke to one of your people in the mall — Nasir. He said he returned it here."

"Sure, we have a wallet. What is your name and address?"

I responded and then he reached down on a shelf below him and came out with my wallet. He handed it to me, and I took it and glanced quickly at its contents. I couldn't believe it. "Thank you, guys, so much for this. Is there anything I can do for you?"

"Just say some good things about us to people you meet," he said, and the rest joined in smiles and laughter.

Outside in the hallway, I looked more carefully. All appeared to be there, and then I checked my two hidden hundred dollar bills. They were both there.

How does one walk and float at the same time? Well, I did it as I headed back to Debbie.

When I reached her, I said, "This is amazing. I can't believe that everything was there. All my cash, and all my credit cards." And then I saw Nasir come into sight. "I have to thank him," I said.

"I turn in things everyday," he said, responding to my effusive thanks. "It's the right thing to do. I spend a lot of time here, and I find a lot."

"Well, I am thrilled you were on duty today."

"I am here seven days a week, ten hours a day."

"Oh my God," I said, "that is an awfully long week. Do you have a family?"

"A wife and three children," he said. "We do need the money."

"Do you have a house or an apartment" I asked.

"We have a small flat that a priest, Father Bradley, helped us to find after Catholic Charities reached out to him. He is a good man."

"My wife works for Catholic Charities," I said, "and we both know Father Bradley." I turned in the direction of Debbie and signaled her to join us.

"Deb, this is Nasir. Thank God, he turned in the wallet, and he was just telling me that Father Bradley has been a big help to him after Catholic Charities helped to make the connection."

"Ah Caritas," she said, and Nasir nodded in affirmation. "Good to meet you. Father Bradley is a good man."

"Yes, he helped to place two of my children in his school, and the other will attend next year. He also found a place for us to live, doesn't cost too much."

"That's wonderful," my wife said. "Have you been here long?"

"Two years. I had my own farm in Pakistan and was doing well. I was happy, but I lost everything because of religious wars. Thank God for Caritas — I had, of course, to leave and start all over." He gave a sigh, and then said, "but because of Caritas and people like Father Bradley, I have work and can take care of my family."

Nasir and Debbie talked a bit more about Catholic Charities and then we said good-bye. As I walked away, I thought of how this day had offered me hope in the simple act of one good man who did the right thing. A man who had had his world ripped away, but had found hope through the efforts of those in Catholic Charities. On this day, he had given me hope in the simple goodness that makes all the difference. And it also opened my eyes once again to the stories in each person's life.

My story had begun in time with a trip to my niece's home, and it ended with my discovery of someone else's story, someone who came from a distant land, found his way, and revealed his character to me with one small gesture.

Poetic Inspirations

The City Squire Ale House

In 1967, I started my teaching career at Notre Dame High School in Schenectady. After a few days of searching, I found a small two-room apartment on Union Street. It so happened that Catholic Charities had its Schenectady office right next door, and the person in charge of the Schenectady office at the time was Father Lou Douglass, who happened to be a friend of my brother, also a priest. In addition to being the director of Catholic Charities, Father Douglass taught English classes at Mater Christi Seminary in Albany. Because I was teaching English and because he was a friend of my brother's, Father Douglass, shortly after I started teaching, offered to take me to dinner and over dinner share a few thoughts about teaching. I eagerly said yes, and so on a Friday night we ended up at the City Squire, the first restaurant I ever dined in in the city of Schenectady. I remember that I felt very comfortable in the small Irish pub with its good food and warm, friendly atmosphere.

For most of my life from that point on living in Schenectady and Niskayuna, the City Squire became one of my favorite places for a beer, some good food, and a warm, welcoming spirit. Then in 2015, the City Squire closed. I had lost an old friend.

So I was thrilled in 2018 when I heard that it was re-opening under new management, and what made it especially exciting was that the new managers were John and Katrina Isopo. I knew them both, and I had actually taught Katrina at Notre Dame-Bishop Gibbons. I wanted to do something special for her and at the same time acknowledge the history of the City Squire. So I spent time at the Schenectady Historical Society, but did not find any relevant information. An administrator, however, suggested that I visit the Archives in City Hall. There I discovered a small gold mine about the history of the restaurant. I found the building permit dated July 23, 1935, and newspaper comments about the pub from its early days. At one point, the archivist wondered if I would be interested in one of the menus for that time. This was pure gold. Then I interviewed some of the old regular patrons and also interviewed the longest running owner of the restaurant, a legend, Rod Riehl. From this historical pursuit and the interviews, I wrote a poem, which I had framed by my niece, a professional framer.

I gave the framed poem to Katrina, and she was very pleased and put it on the wall of the restaurant. One year later, Karina and her husband decided to turn the management over to another team, but the poem remained. In the poem, which now hangs on the wall along the far side of the bar, I try to capture the history and the flavor of the restaurant.

THE CITY SQUIRE ALE HOUSE

On July 23, 1935
A building permit
for "a store and dwelling"
at 1018 Keyes Avenue.
What rose
was John Meaney's Grill
a place where neighbors and locals
were welcomed:
high school students
for a sandwich or snack
the local gas station owner
for a cool beverage after work
a politician eager
to discuss the future
of Schenectady.
And ah, the prices:
"Egg Salad Sandwich — 15 cents."
"Full Course Chicken Dinner — 1 dollar."
"A Dobler Lager — 10 cents."

Names change with owners
and so
John Meaney's Grill
became Keyes Avenue Tap Room
and then Hogan's City Squire Restaurant,
and then The City Squire.

But always constant and vibrant
was the welcoming spirit
captured best in the words
of long-time owner Rod Riehl,
"We became a place
for regulars and families
who celebrated moments of joy
and gathered at times of sadness."
And the bagpipes played on
But
Moments of disruption came too
like the 1973 fire
and then the words in 2015,
"The City Squire is closed."

Yet irrepressible
were the memories
of friends and families and traditions
and laughter, good food, and song.
And so it was just a matter of time
before someone
felt a pulse
and touched the memories.
And now 1015 Keyes Avenue
once again rings
with laughter, good food, and song
at the City Squire Ale House.

Jordan

I have written about the unexpected death of Notre Dame-Bishop Gibbons senior Jordan Baumes in narrative form in *Voices from Room 6*. Jordan was a superb basketball player and a good student. As sometimes happens in life, light can be followed by great darkness: on the day of the car accident, Jordan had received an excellent scholarship to play basketball at Bard College. The following days were filled with sadness at the school. In my English classroom, a friend of Jordan's left five long-stemmed roses on the desk where Jordan sat. The roses remained there for maybe two weeks, and then I took them and put them in a vase on the mantle behind my desk. Before I put them up, I cut four of the roses to an appropriate size for the vase, but I left one longer so that it stood out in the vase. I then wrote the following poem and tacked it just below the vase of roses.

ONE STAR

Often during an intense moment
Under the boards
A hand would rise above the rest
Not the hand of the tallest on the floor
But the tallest hand
And the basketball player would
Come back down with the ball.
I'd like to think that for Jordan
It was one of those shining moments
When he reached for the stars.
In our hallway at Gibbons
He was among the tallest
And even taller if he decided
To do something with his red hair.
They say that red-haired people
Are passionate and committed
And for Jordan, you could add,
Especially on the basketball court,
A fierce competitiveness and fire.
And then there was his smile
And the whole way he looked at you
As if to say, "Don't worry, it'll be ok.
We'll get it done."

On the first day of school this year
He wrote that the best moment
In his high school career
Was "My 93 on the English Regents."
His friends have spoken in simple eloquence
About what he meant to them
About what a friend he was
And how they intend to keep his memory alive.
Jordan — the smiling red-haired student
Who leapt above the rest
And became a star.

Fire at the Top

Looking back now at the one-year span, it was pretty impressive, actually a great accomplishment in a one-year span. In the fall of 2017, fire decimated the ND-BG Field House and rocked the football program. One year later, Holy Trinity, composed of students from ND-BG, Catholic Central in Troy, and Saratoga Catholic, was competing in the State Finals at the Syracuse Dome. Almost literally out of the ashes, the Holy Trinity Pride rose up and created a success story with talent, grit, tenaciousness, spirit, and, not to be redundant, pride.

The immediate outpouring of generosity after the fire was extraordinary and allowed the Holy Trinity Pride to play in their first sectional game ever two days after the fire. So much given by so many people: local universities donating uniforms and helmets, area high schools donating cleats and shoulder pads, equipment companies donating helmets, friends of the school donating money, food, and water. One saw the best in people. Though the team lost the Sectional game to Hoosick Valley 46-12, the seeds had been planted in all those returning to the program to make 2018 an outstanding season. In losing so much in the fire, and also losing the game, they had begun to enkindle their own fire.

After an early season loss to Mechanicville, the Pride went on a win-streak behind an outstanding offense and a strong, quick defense. In the Section II Class C Championship, Holy Trinity's Joe Tortello threw four touchdown passes, two to Nacier Hundley and two to Noah Foster, to lead the Pride to a 34 - 12 victory. After a quarterfinal win over Ogdensburg Free Academy, Holy Trinity faced Burke Catholic in the State Semi-final.

I drove down to Middletown, New York, for the game. It was rainy and on the cold side, as I recall. What stood out for me in the pre-game period was the size and precision of the Bishop Burke team. They outnumbered our players 2 to 1, and their drills were military-like. I said to myself, "Well, this may be the end of the road for us." Though we took an early lead —7-0 — and held it at half-time, we fell behind in the third quarter and entered the fourth quarter trailing 17-7. The rain kept falling.

Then the tide shifted. A touchdown run by Kiser, and two touchdown passes by Tortello, one to Foster and one to Hundley, put the Pride ahead. And then clinging to a tight lead late in the fourth quarter, magic happened. On a third down and fifteen from our own 30, Tortello fired a short pass over the middle to Jordan Mettier, who pitched the ball back to Nacier Hundley who covered some turf, and then pitched back to Nelon Priest who ran until he was stopped on the Burke 46. It was first down, and the Pride was able to run out the clock.

We waited until the players came off the field and then walked down to where the celebration was taking place. As I watched the hugs and handshakes, I knew that something special had taken place on the field. The second half had shifted the stage to Burke, and I was not alone in thinking that the game was over. Yet, the team had never given up, and that made the day very special. When I got home, I sat at my desk and wrote this poem:

PRIDE ROSE TO THE CHALLENGE

On a cold and overcast day
Holy Trinity gathered pre-game
somewhat haphazardly it appeared
near the far end zone.
The players, uniformed in white,
seemed
to move in slow motion —
no clarifying patterns
forecasting success.
To the right
stretching out for almost 40 yards
the Eagles of Bishop Burke —
in gun metal gray —
used the yardage stripes
as tightropes for their execution
of precision
in numbers far exceeding
their Trinity opponent.

Yet Holy Trinity
on this cold grey day
managed through grit and will
to take a 7-0 lead
into the locker room.
Would the lead hold?
Could the depleted Pride
be able to withstand
the overwhelming forces?

The second half brought icy rain
and ignited the Eagle offense
as they scored one touchdown
and then another.
Shoulders sagged in the bleachers.
Looks of defeat and sadness
spread across the crowd.
'Well, it was a great year" —
the emerging thought
among the Trinity faithful.

And then Holy Trinity
found something in themselves:
"It isn't over!"
"We aren't done!"
"Let's go, Pride!"
With magic, dazzle, and grace
tenaciousness and fire
They rose to the occasion,
scored three touchdowns,
stopped the Eagles,
and then with two sensational first downs
closed out the clock.

It was a day to remember
when a small group of determined athletes
showed us all
what it means
to have Pride.

There was one game left, for the State Championship, against Skaneateles. The game was thrilling, but we lost 28-25. The team, of course, was heart-broken, and I felt for each one. I had a sense of how tough it was to have come so far and not to have gotten the golden ring, but, for me, that cold, grey, rainy day in Middletown when it looked as if the season was over and then to see the tide shift, the spirit rise, and have us emerge victorious was the moment to treasure.

Leo

My older brother Leo in many ways shaped the direction of my life. Because of him, I decided not to join the Navy and apply to college. Through the college years, he always seemed to show up at crucial times — to take me out to dinner or a show, to send me a check at times when I had no money. He was the reason I got the job in the school where I spent 47 years teaching because he was good friends with the principal just as I was leaving graduate school and the high school was losing an English teacher. When I almost gave up teaching, he encouraged me to persevere by recalling his own difficult years as a young Catholic priest. As I have journeyed through life, he has remained a strong presence, a light of hope and direction.

During his later years, he developed pretty severe neuropathy and began to rely on a series of aids — cane, walker, motor scooter, wheel chair, adjustable chair. Still he remained mentally sharp, taking courses like Learning Hebrew, and figuring out ways, with the help of his parishioners, to continue to say Mass. Even in his senior years, he has remained a role model and a beacon. On his 88th birthday, he arranged a small party (16 good friends) for himself, and at the party I read this poem as a tribute to him.

MOVING ALONG WITH LEO

What is a number anyway,
I mean, take the number 88, for example
Just two snowmen standing around
Chatting about the weather.
So consider what the number zero said to
        the number eight —
"Nice belt," he said, and eight blushed —
Just a couple of guys with nice belts.
I mean if you apply the number to age
it's only two times forty four
And though 88 means that you may have
        lived as long
as anyone in your family
Still it doesn't have to take on an
        overbearing significance.

True, time can slow one down just a bit.
Maybe you can't skip down the stairs
        the way you used to
Or play a snappy game of ping pong,
But the mind compensates — works out
routines — what to do, for example,
        if you have an early morning
meeting — and it takes you a
        long time to get ready ?
Solution — for this man — shower at
        night and then wear to bed
what you are wearing to the event —
Wake up — Just a little brush of the hair,
some shoes — and Voila — you are ready.

And let's say, for example, that you wish to
*   continue to celebrate Mass*
though you have slowed down a bit physically
well, for this man — create a system with the help
*   of so many good people —*
People like
Don, Ruth, Elizabeth, Mary, Marcia , Rosemarie
*   and many others*
And try this approach: with their help.
Scooter to the front door, walker to the car;
at the Church — the transfer chair right up to the altar:
walker at the altar for all essential duties,
Transfer chair to give out communion,
*   and processing out.*
A system that works — you just have to think it out
and rely on some wonderful people.

And what else is there that helps one to engage
*   with the number 88.*
For this man, let's try two vital ingredients: the first
— the desire to learn something new each day
from taking a course in Hebrew to listening
*   to the stories of others*
to reading book after book after book
accompanied with the passion to share
*   what he has learned.*

— *And the second ingredient is a sense of humor. If*
you get a good joke, you can tell it until
the cows come home, as this man occasionally
does — like the one about the golfer looking at the
hole and saying, "No question, I can reach the green
in two." But when he swings his club, he miscal-
culates slightly and drives the ball into the woods.
From the woods the golfer looks out at the green
from under a limb and says to himself, "I can still
reach the green in two." But when he swings, the
ball rockets into the limb, ricochets back, and hits
the golfer in the forehead killing him. Shortly after,
the golfer stands in front of St. Peter, and St. Peter
looks at him and says, "I see you play a little golf,"
and the golfer says, "I got here in two."

Watching the reactions of people to a joke
can be a joy,
but really the more one thinks about it
the more one realizes that though some humor can
depend on a story
with a twist or a surprise ending, the real
spirit of humor, and it's so true for this man,
comes in his ability to laugh at life's absurdities
to keep things in perspective, to be able to
laugh at himself
and thus keep a balance and an equilibrium.

Yes, there are moments of doubt —
Sometimes one can almost give in to a feeling of sadness
for self, envying what others have:
for example, when this man looks out his window
and sees someone his own age walking easily
    and confidently toward a destination — for a moment
    he wishes that he had what the other person has —
    the ability to walk gracefully and with confidence,
but he pauses and wonders what struggles
    the other person
might have
and how hard his road might be.

And then he reflects on the myriad ways
he has been graced and blessed,
with so many good people and so many opportunities
and he smiles and he sits back in his chair
and remembers what the singer says:

"Now I think of my life as vintage wine
From fine old kegs
From the brim to the dregs
As it pours sweet and clear
"You know what" he says to himself
"88 will be a very good year."

Dolores Scheuer, Teacher

Dolores Scheuer, math teacher, mother, and friend, was a colleague for over 30 years at Notre Dame and then Notre Dame-Bishop Gibbons School. The students often called her "Ma" or "Mom" because of her motherly instincts. A few salient qualities that marked her character were a rollicking sense of humor, a quiet courage, and an infinite amount of patience. I still laugh when I recall the time she removed a condom from the handle of a water fountain, held it up, and said, "Who keeps putting balloons on these handles?" When another teacher and I had fallen out of favor with the principal and he was not allowing speeches about us at graduation on our twenty-fifth anniversary as teachers, she stepped to the podium for other business and then segued into a salute of each of us. The principal just stared straight ahead. Math class with Dolores was always charged with her sense of humor — she could tease the students, and they could tease her, but always with respect.

Late one afternoon well into my teaching career, I headed down the hallway, weary after a full day. I passed Dolores' room, and there she was sitting at a desk working. She looked up, smiled, and asked me the same question she had asked me one afternoon in my first year of teaching.

HOW YA DOING?

It's getting kind of late
and so you gather your jacket
and bag and thermos
and start down the hall
weary, worn down
by the day.
You reach the doorway
to Room 5
and you glance in.
A teacher looks up
from a student desk
where she's been working —
maybe correcting a paper
or editing the yearbook —
and she says,
"How ya doing?"
You smile and say,
"Not bad, still trying
to keep it rolling."
She laughs and the weight
on your back eases up a bit.
"How ya doing?"
You look at her.
She's got to be weary too
and tired, in the late
afternoon of this day.

On the lawn behind her
the water from the sprinkler
dances in the sun's light
And your eyes return
to the smile on her face.
You chat for a few moments
about colleagues and students
and her new granddaughter — Nina —
and how this new life will keep
her and Ed so busy.
You laugh again
about an old teaching friend
who moved out west
and then it's time to go,
"See ya, Dolores."

As you continue on down
the quiet, clean hallway,
you think of this woman,
this colleague, this friend,
and it dawns on you
that her question
"How ya doing"
is one she asked you
many years ago
late one afternoon
when you were just starting
to teach.

You have reached the front door
and you step out
into the warm late afternoon sun.
The world is still except for
the sound of water wisping over the ground.
You breathe in the air deeply
And then you smile and say,
"Thanks, Dolores."

Films That Mattered

When I first started teaching English in the 60's, the main focus of English class was literature, grammar, and writing. Occasionally, I might show short films that connected thematically to certain texts. Once in a great while, I would have a feature length film of a play by Shakespeare, for example, *Hamlet* or *Macbeth*. In the early 70's, I developed a course called "Introduction to Film," in which we spent some time learning the language of film and analyzing a number of short films.

Over my years of teaching English, film became more and more a vital part of my teaching. I think that at the heart of the matter, film directly connected to my whole sense of art. Its purpose is not only to elevate the soul and mind, but also to inform and build a community of understanding and appreciation. I felt the same way about certain films that I felt about pieces of literature that had touched my soul and I hoped also the souls and minds of those I taught. I wanted to share that experience with others and explore together how a work came to be so accomplished. In the written texts, there are those moments that catch the life-blood of the text: Biff Loman saying at the "Requiem" for his father, "I know who I am"; And Blanche Dubois's words to the doctor who is about to take her to the institution, "Whoever you are, I have always depended on the kindness of strangers." Films have those defining moments too. Films also have the power, the beauty, and the insight into human nature to transform and lift us all and help us see life more clearly.

In my senior film elective, I often had the students make a list of their top ten films, based on their film experience up to that point in their life. They loved doing it, but what made it an especially meaningful experience was when they had a chance to read their list, and suddenly there were all kinds of comments coming about the lists being shared: "Oh, my God, I loved that film — totally forgot about it." "That's on my list too!" "Really, you like that film that much?" It was a good way to start a unit on film. The second task I asked students to do in the early stages of the course was to choose one moment from a film that would remain indelibly marked on their minds forever. I gave them about 10 minutes to describe the moment they selected. Then we shared. I can't think of a more exciting time in the classroom than when kids are eager to hear each other speak about something that is very special to them. With both the top ten list and a moment one would never forget, I too shared with the students.

Sometimes in the past when I have been with friends and the subject of movies has come up, I like to know what films they love and why. I use a line I have stolen from sports' shows — "Name your Mount Rushmore of basketball players" — and say, "Name your Mount Rushmore of Movies." Friends usually pause and really think for a moment or two. Sometimes, I give my four to get the ball rolling. So here are my four films, all of relatively equal stature though for different reasons.

The Graduate

The year is 1967, and I had just started teaching. I guess, in a way, I identified with the central character, Benjamin Braddock, played by Dustin Hoffman, heading home after graduating college. I was hooked from the opening scene: a close-up of Ben on his flight and then his exit from the airport as the camera follows him on a walking sidewalk to the music of Simon and Garfunkel's "Sounds of Silence." At the welcome home party for him given by his parents, we see Ben trying to navigate through all those who have a plan for him. For example, Mr. Maguire, a somewhat pompous friend of his father's, who takes Ben aside and with his arm around Ben, says, "I just want to say one word to you." Ben looks baffled. "Plastics," Maguire says, "there is a great future in plastics." Mike Nichols, the director, was certainly nightmarishly prophetic.

Shortly after that scene, Ben retreats to his den for a moment of peace when the sophisticated and beguiling Mrs. Robinson (Anne Bancroft), wife of Ben's father's law partner, enters the room and begins what is a wonderful comic scene concluding with Mrs. Robinson talking Ben into driving her home. The relationship grows into a summer of escapades with Mrs. Robinson while at home Ben spends time floating in the pool. "What are you doing?" his father asks. And Ben responds, "Well, I guess I am just drifting." In a brilliant sequence, Mike Nichols uses a series of montages to take the viewer from hotel bedroom with Ben and Mrs. Robinson to Ben drifting in the pool while "Hello Darkness" serves as the unifying musical motif.

Life grows more complicated when Ben's parents urge Ben to call Elaine (Katherine Ross), the daughter of Mrs. Robinson, and ask her out. Against Mrs. Robinson's demand that Ben not do that, Ben does and then life grows complicated and dark. Through the great direction, outstanding musical support, and the acting of Hoffman, Ross, and Bancroft, the movie builds to a a wonderfully comic and dramatic ending.

Mike Nickols frames *The Graduate* with the song "Sounds of Silence," which was a brilliant touch on his part. In the opening scene on the plane, Ben appeared to be kind of expressionless, almost dazed. In the final scene, after Elaine and Ben have broken through the silence and reached each other, the look on their faces at the back of the bus changes from smiles to expressions very close to Ben's look in the first scene. The viewer is left with questions and concerns about their future together, but given the barriers they have broken through, it seems to be just the right look.

Bonnie and Clyde

I remember leaving the Troy Theater on River Street in silence. Actually it may have been the quietest exiting crowd from a movie I've ever experienced. You knew the ending was coming, but you didn't want it to happen. The way Arthur Penn shot the final scene, you are almost frozen as you watch the exquisitely executed death scene: the final glances of Bonnie and Clyde at each other knowing what is imminent; and then the rain of bullets far, far beyond what was necessary creating a dance of death in their riddled bodies.

Amidst the dreariness of the Depression years, Clyde Barrow (just out of prison) shows up in Bonnie Parker's world of waitressing in a one-horse town and offers her an option: Come with me and be a bank robber or stay and die of boredom. And we are off into the fictionalized story of two real life villains. In the early action, the bank heists come across as kind of keystone cops episodes, and then everything turns when Clyde shoots the bank manager who has run out of the bank and jumped on the running board of Clyde's car. Two major shootouts follow, one in which everyone manages to escape from a motel against the overwhelming odds of a large number of Texas Rangers; the second, in a meadow when the Barrow gang is surrounded again by Rangers. Clyde and Bonnie are both shot, but with C.W. Moss, they manage to escape the trap. Clyde's brother, Buck Barrow, played by Gene Hackman, dies surrounded by Rangers in a harrowing scene, while Blanche (Estelle Parsons), his wife, blinded by a shot to the head, screams and screams.

We know the climax is coming: Bonnie and Clyde will not make it, but before the final horrific scene, Bonnie writes a ballad celebrating their lives and concluding with their demise, "Some day they'll go down together / and they'll bury them side by side / To few it'll be grief, to the law a relief / But it's death for Bonnie and Clyde."

After Bonnie reads the poem to Clyde, he is overwhelmed and says, "You made me a hero." What follows is their first sexual consummation.

We know what is coming, and though emotionally we realize that we have been set up to feel the loss, it still hits like a thousand bricks. And the rest is silence.

There is so much in the silence of the audience. The editing and direction of this scene is so artfully done that one cannot help but feel intensely for the lives lost. True, the actors are attractive and appealing. True, the cards are stacked against them — a trap has been set. Still what is elevated here in this incredible death scene is the value of life, pure and simple.

The Shawshank Redemption

Shawshank lingers in your soul and becomes part of you. Perhaps the essence of what lingers is best captured in the words of Andy (Tim Robbins) as he speaks to Red (Morgan Freeman) in the prison yard: "Remember, Red, hope is a good thing, maybe the best of things, and no good thing ever dies." Earlier Red had told Andy in the dining room that "Hope is a very dangerous thing, my friend, it can kill a man." The movie proves Andy right.

What does one do when one is convicted of a double murder and sentenced to life in prison, a murder that one did not commit? You can hope. With a small rock hammer that Andy procures from Red to pursue his interest in sculpting, Andy's journey begins. What makes his journey so affecting is that we see his struggle through the eyes of Red. And what especially characterizes Andy is his ability to instill hope through his intelligence. Sometimes we can see a plan being laid out, but in Andy's case we and Red can only see it darkly and only in time do we see what he has been doing all along. He says to Red at one point that it all comes down to one choice: "Get busy living or get busy dying."

In a friendship, one does not forget the other. Andy tells Red that he dreams of someday living in Mexico, in the coastal town of Zihuatanejo. He also tells Red that if Red should ever get out of prison that he should travel to a particular site, an old tree near a stone wall, where he first made love to his wife. At this site, there is a package for Red.

As Red, having been released from prison, rides a bus to Mexico on his way to find Andy who had escaped by using that small chisel (20 year effort) to carve out a hole in the wall, Red says, "I hope I can make it across the border, I hope to see my friend and shake his hand, I hope the Pacific is as blue as it has been in my dreams. I hope."

The Shawshank Redemption is primarily a character study and, as the title suggests, is about the act of saving one's self and others; it is also about the act of regaining a life after much suffering — in Andy Dufresne's case when there was no crime. Against great odds, Andy showed Red a way, a way that was marked by hope. Yes, "Too long a sacrifice can make a stone of the heart," but a long sacrifice with a goal burning deep within and a plan to achieve this goal can make the heart in the end fill with joy.

Nightjohn

The final film on my Mount Rushmore was a difficult choice. Five years ago, if someone had asked me, I would have said, *Midnight Cowboy,* a tough, heart-breaking story of friendship starring Jon Voight and Dustin Hoffman. It is a great study of character, but one other movie now has risen above it for me because of its themes of sacrifice, raw courage, and grit. And I had the opportunity to see the effect the movie *Nightjohn* had on my students over a number of years. *Nightjohn* is the story of a slave who had reached freedom but returned to the South to teach others how to read. The principal beneficiary of his teaching is Sarny, a young slave girl whose relationship with John forms the heart of the film.

Nightjohn is about reading and about words. John begins to teach Sarny late one night after he has entered the hovel where the slaves are kept and sees that Sarny is still awake. He asks for tobacco and she audaciously says, "What you got to trade?" His response is "Letters. I know letters." And when she asks him if he can teach her to read, he says that first you need to know letters. She shares a small pinch of tobacco. He starts his lesson with the letter A, which he draws on the dirt floor, and he says, "The letter A can stand on its own two feet."

What makes this action so heroic is that John is going against a system in which slaves are not allowed to read. When John is challenged by the Old Man among the slaves who says "What are words anyway," John responds, "Words are freedom, Old Man, cause that's all things are made of — words, laws, deeds, passes, all they are is words. White ·folks got all the words, and they mean to keep them. You get some words for yourself — and you'll be free."

You find yourself drawn to John — I don't think I have ever watched an actor who made me feel that he was more into the character than Carl Lumbly who plays John. In his desire to teach Sarny how to read, he is emblematic of the concept of a hero, not Joseph Campbell's hero who goes on an adventure and comes home changed, as Odysseus does, but a hero who enters a world and changes it.

When John suffers the fate of someone who has attempted to teach others to read, his last words to Sarny are, "Old Man say that when you lose one hand, the other one gets stronger. You the other hand now, Girl. You know what you got to do."

When the other slaves ask Sarny what John wrote in the dirt before he was dragged away after having two fingers chopped off, she tells them, "John, it be John."

Nightjohn is the story of a teacher who shows others the way out of darkness, and the special beauty of the story is in the faces of John and his student Sarny as we witness the passing of the torch. Film elevates the reading of that story.

Three Great Moments in Films

There are moments in film that are indelibly marked on our minds. Here are three very special moments for me. One speaks of the spiritual link between characters, one speaks of an adversarial relationship, and the third is about how one character discovers a world that will transform him.

The Killing Fields

The Killing Fields is about the fall of Cambodia to the radical Khmer Rouge and the coverage of the story by *New York Times* journalist Sydney Schanberg (Sam Waterson) with the help of Dith Pran (Dr. Haing S Ngor), a native of Cambodia and also a journalist. Once the Khmer Rouge has taken over, the world becomes precarious for all foreigners, and escape is crucial. Though Pran is able to get his family out, he chooses to stay with Schanberg. Then they are caught. Through a series of heart-throbbing close calls and some brilliantly executed persuasion via translation by Dith Pran, Schanberg gets out, but Pran fails to get out when the fake passport that has been created for him is discovered, and he disappears into the slave camps of the

Khmer Rouge. What we see in this first major segment of the movie is the bond between Schanberg and Pran. What follows in the second half of the movie is Pran's heroic effort to survive the brutal life imposed on him and by extension millions of others by the Khmer Rouge.

Back in the United States, Schanberg, haunted by the thought that Pran helped him to escape but didn't make it out himself, searches for evidence of Pran's survival but to no avail. Pran, however, through intelligence, tenacity, and grit, has managed to survive many harrowing experiences. One day, having escaped a village attacked by the Khmer Rouge, he staggers into a Red Cross camp located near the border of Thailand.

News reaches Schanberg that Pran is alive, and Schanberg informs Pran's family in New York and then catches a flight for Thailand. It is in the moment when they meet that so much is revealed: especially the character of Dith Pran.

Dith Pran is caring for a young boy who has suffered a leg wound when he is told that there is someone to see him. He gets up and walks toward the open doorway, and just as he exits we hear John Lennon's "Imagine" start to play. The camera is on Pran's face, then we cut to Schanberg getting out of the back seat of a car and looking toward Pran. Schanberg steps out and starts to walk toward Pran. "Imagine there's no country," Lennon sings. And then the camera pulls back from Pran's face and we see him walk right to left toward Schanberg. "Nothing to kill or die for," sings Lennon, and then Pran starts running toward Schanberg and leaps into his arms. Schanberg turns around once with Pran in his arms. We have a long shot showing them embracing. We cut to a group of young natives watching the reunion. Then back to a two-shot of Schanberg with his arms on Pran's shoulders saying, "Do you forgive me?" And the camera cuts to Pran who says, "Nothing to forgive. Nothing." And Lennon's words as the two men hug again, "I hope some day you'll join us, and the world will be as one."

Searching for Bobby Fischer

Searching for Bobby Fischer is the story of a young boy, Josh Waitzkin, and his journey from a simple, instinctive love of the game of chess into the feverish and intense world of competitive chess. Josh is a chess prodigy, and the film is adapted from a true story written by Fred Waitzkin about his son's love of and success at the game.

The movie captures your heart from the beginning with Fred (played by Joe Montegna) discovering something that his wife Bonnie (played by Joan Allen) has known for some time — that their son Josh, wonderfully played by Max Pomeranc, is very good at the game of chess. Of course, no one has meant more to the game of chess than the brilliant, eccentric Bobbie Fischer, and his role in the film is both as a role model for Josh and a foil for Josh because of Josh's very nature. The title refers to the fact that Bobbie Fischer has disappeared from the world of chess, and the question looms — will he return and if not, will we find another Bobbie Fischer?

The world of chess oscillates between the world of exuberance and free flow and the world of sober and studied play. In Washington Square Park, Josh becomes friends with Vinnie (played by Lawrence Fishburne), who is a master of speed chess. At home, Josh is instructed by the disciplined Bruce Pandolfini (Ben Kingsley), who has been hired by Josh's dad. Bruce knows the history of chess and every move Bobbie Fischer ever made. Bruce sees the opponent one faces as someone one must have contempt for. This attitude strikes at the heart of Josh, who refuses to give in to this attitude. Bruce says at one point, "Bobbie Fischer held the world in contempt." Josh counters, "I'm not him."

The movie culminates in a championship match between Josh and another young prodigy, Jonathan Poe (played by Michael Nuremberg), who scares the life out of Josh. The night before the match, Josh admits that he is scared and says to Bruce, "I can't beat him." Bruce says that you may be right, but that he has never been so proud of anyone in his life, "I am proud to call myself your teacher." The match itself is an extended moment that will remain always in my mind.

The game is played on an elevated level at the far end of a room filled with chess matches going on. Jonathan is already seated and waiting as Josh enters the room. Josh takes a seat, and each boy stares at the other. The match begins, and we cut to an adjacent room where Josh's parents, Bruce, and Vinnie are watching the match on a monitor. At about the fourth move, Josh has a chance to bring his Queen out, a move encouraged by Vinnie as part of a free-wheeling type of game, but a move thought of as foolish by Bruce. Josh brings out his Queen, and Bruce says, "Oh, Jesus." Within four moves, Josh has lost his Queen. The camera comes in close on Josh, and we see concern. Vinnie says, "Josh is setting him up." The game continues, and Josh makes some deft moves, at one point freezing Jonathan with a move and adding a line Jonathan had used on an old man in the park, "Trick or treat."

The match continues and the camera cuts back and forth between the faces and the hands of the boys as the pieces hit the board like hammers. At one point Jonathan makes a move, and the camera freezes the frame of the chessboard and then cuts to Bruce who says, "That was a mistake." The camera moves to a close-up of Josh's face, and we hear Bruce's voice-over, "Look deep, Josh, it's there. It's twelve moves away, but it's there. You've got him." And the voice-over continues, just barely audible, with the camera on Josh's face. "Don't move until you see it," Bruce says, and then we are in a moment from the past when Bruce had said the same thing, and Josh had responded, "I can't see it." And Bruce said, "Let me make it easier for you" and swept the board clean of pieces with his right forearm. In the present the camera is floor level when the pieces come flying off the board. Josh looks left as if he still remembers — we see a now empty hall — and Johnathan looks strangely at him. Then Josh studies the board and finally his eyes light on the black pawn in front of the white bishop, and we see Bruce say, "He's got it."

Josh looks at Jonathan, and Jonathan says, "What?" Josh stares at him. "Come on, move," Josh stares and then puts out his right hand. Jonathan says, "What's that supposed to mean?" Cut to Vinnie who asks the same question. Bruce says, "He's offering him a draw." Josh says, "I'm offering you a draw."

Jonathan says, "Draw, you've got to be kidding." Josh's hand comes down, and he says, "You've lost and just don't know it." Jonathan, "I've lost?" Josh, "Look at the board." Jonathan, "I have." Josh, "Take the draw and we share the championship. Take the draw." Jonathan, "Move!"

And play resumes, first Jonathan stands, and then both boys are standing in rapid-fire play, as pieces disappear from the board. And then Josh's pawn becomes a Queen, and he says, "Check." Jonathan makes one more move to protect his King, and Josh's next move is Checkmate. Jonathan stares at the board, and then tips over his King. Camera cuts to Josh who says, "Good Game." Jonathan stares at him, nods slightly, turns and walks away.

What is undeniable in the character of Josh is his decency, even to those who had in a way sneered at him before. He will not, as Bobbie Fischer did, hold contempt in his heart for others. Through a dramatic and brilliantly orchestrated climatic scene, Josh remains true to himself.

Almost Famous

It is important to establish that the film *Almost Famous* is written and directed by Cameron Crowe because the movie is really his story, a semi-autobiographical account of a teen-age journalist, William Miller, touring with a rock band named Stillwater. Crowe himself toured as a journalist in the 70's with a number of rock bands, including Led Zeppelin and Lynyrd Skynyrd. In his glowing review of the movie, Roger Ebert captured the essence succinctly when he said, "Oh, what a lovely film."

When I think of this movie that I view so highly, I can cite several moments that stand out and glow. For example, the scene on the bus after the band has experienced a bad gig and the entire troupe is lower than a snake's belly. Elton John's "Tiny Dancer" comes across the sound system and one band member joins in, then a few more, and as the song reaches a crescendo all are singing — a wonderful illustration of the power of music to lift the spirit. But the moment that I have selected occurs earlier in the film.

Michael Angarano plays the younger William Miller, and it is a scene with him that I will discuss. After Elaine, his mom played by Frances McDormand, has created a stifling home atmosphere that Anita, his older sister, can no longer live in — much of it has to do with Anita's choice of music — she decides to leave home and become a flight attendant.

"This song explains why I'm leaving home to become a stewardess," says Anita as she puts Simon and Garfunkel's "America" on the record player. She stares at her mother, and the scene shifts to the front lawn with Anita and her boyfriend packing the car. The music continues and eleven year old William stands in front of this Mom watching his sister prepare to leave. At one moment Anita walks up to her brother, bends over, looks directly in his eyes, and says, "One day, you'll be cool." Then she pulls him close, and in his ear, says, "Look under your bed. It'll set you free."

Departure over, we are in William's bedroom, and in a high angle shot we see that he is reaching under his bed and pulling out a bag. Side shot of William opening bag, and then a close-up of contents: a stack of albums, the first "The Beach Boys Pet Sounds." Then a medium shot at normal angle of William as he starts flipping through the albums. Camera back into close-up, slightly high angle of titles: *Led Zeppelin, Neil Young, Jimmy Hendrix, Cream, Joni Mitchell* — William runs his fingers affectionately across a number of covers; then he looks puzzled for a second by the Bob Dylan album — the music "America" has stopped — and then he flips Dylan to find *Tommy the Who* turned sideways. He turns it right side up and opens it to find a note inside: "Listen to *Tommy* with a candle burning and you will see your entire future." William carefully places the album on the record player, lifts the arm with the needle in an extreme close-up, and the needle hits the record to Tommy's "Sparks." Music and the camera backs to a medium shot of William standing trying to absorb the music. High angle shot of album spinning and then a dissolve into a superimposition of William lighting a candle as the music spins. We have a side shot of William as he leans back, a little smile crosses his face and the superimposition holds for a few seconds showing William, the music spinning, and the candle. And then in a second dissolve — music still playing — we see a blue denim cloth with names in graffiti — Black Sabbath, William, Lester Bangs, large lettering of Led Zelleplin, and a pen finishing the N in Zelleplin. We are in a high school classroom with William Miller, set free into the world of music.

William's life is transformed by music. In many ways, the literature I have read — and shared in the classroom — has transformed me. The novels, plays, poetry, and essays I have been blessed to read have expanded and deepened my understanding and appreciation of human nature and the world we live in. So too have films spoken to me in visual eloquence about the darkness and light in our souls. What Joseph Conrad says about the task of the writer can also fit the task of the filmmaker: "…to make you hear, to make you feel — it is, before all, to make you see."

Style

Bob pressed his foot on the gas pedal and slid under the light as it turned red. Checking the rear-view mirror, he watched the next two cars run the red light. "I don't believe this crap! Someone has got to do something about this stuff." He shifted into his Walter Mitty hero role.

He pulled over to let the two cars go by, and then he hit the switch that lit up the swirling red demon on his roof. He gunned the engine and quickly closed in on them. They slowed and then the lead car eased to the side of the road, followed by the second car. Reaching into the back seat, he grabbed his blue hat with the word POLICE in gold across the front. This would be easy — two birds with one stone.

He had jacked up the fine big time for those two losers, and then he was back on the road again. When he saw the sign EAT, his favorite diner, he began to relax and felt good that someone had left him a parking spot right in front of the place. Probably for a job well done. Looking at his watch, he noticed that it was just a little after 6:00, and his hair appointment wasn't until 7:30. Time for some good food. Yes, his favorite seat was open at the counter, right in front of the dessert shelves, where slanted mirrors doubled the number of giant triple-layered cakes, thick cheesecakes with cherry and blueberry toppings, and chocolate pies with whipped cream that was three inches high. Bob rarely ordered a dessert, but he liked to look.

He needed a coffee to start and had just taken a sip when Walt Wagner, a regular at the diner, plopped down next to him, uttered a big sigh, and then said "Whatcha say, young feller?"

"Heh, Walt, how's it going?" Bob looked at Walt and was struck by the bright red baseball hat with the words "Racquet Fever" emblazoned across the front. "Been playing a little tennis, Walt," Bob said.

Walt chuckled and then took off the hat, exposing his totally bald head. He held the hat out for admiration.

"How about this hat! I'll tell ya, see, I'm up there at the mall in Clifton Park — where they have a store, nothing but hats. Well, I went in and looked all around, and then this one jumped out at me. I liked that line — 'Racquet Fever.' I tried it on, and it fit like a glove." He turned the hat around and placed it back on his head, giving it a slight adjustment.

Bob took a sip of his coffee and then said, "Ever hit the tennis courts?"

"Nah, only exercise I get is walking over here to the diner twice a day. You know — with the Mrs. gone — Lord, be good to her — I come over here for the cooking, not quite as good as home, but close. And where is your little woman tonight?"

"Coffee, Walter?" the waitress said, a warm smile spreading across her face.

"Sounds good, Tina. Is it a fresh pot?"

"Always, Walter, when you are here, always." She looked at Bob and winked.

"The Mrs. out tonight?" Walter asked.

"The good wife — she's in Baltimore for a few days."

"Got some relatives down there? Thanks, Tina."

"No, no relatives down there. Rita's at some big conference, ahh let's see, oh yeah, something about employee relation mediation — something like that."

"Nothing against your wife, young fella, but those words leave me behind." Walter had picked up a menu. "I don't know why I look at this menu. I get the same thing every Friday night — grilled tuna with tomato."

"I think I'll try the scrod — Friday, a good fish night."

· · · · ·

Bob's dinner was delicious. A cup of chicken pastina soup, salad with Italian dressing, and a piece of scrod that screamed out for a larger plate, making Tina's cry of "whale up front" seem fitting when she shouted it through the window into the kitchen, and a baked potato that Bob lathered with butter. And the coffee kept coming.

Walter was rubbing his stomach. "Just can't eat the way I used to. "Tina," —who was sitting at the end of the counter looked up — "Tina, can you fix the rest of this to go, and maybe a little more coffee. Thanks, hon."

Tina took Walt's dish in one hand, and looked at Bob's empty plate, "Wow, you are one hungry dude tonight."

"I'll have the rest of mine to go also," Bob said, and they all laughed as Tina picked the empty plate up.

"Well, Bob, whatcha got on for tonight? A little card game or something?'

"No," Bob glanced at this watch, "actually, I've got an appointment to get my hair cut in about half an hour."

"An appointment? For a haircut? You?"

'Yup," Bob said and laughed. "You know, you gotta make an appointment these days. Rita made this one for me last week."

"Where is this barbershop located?"

"Over in Latham — place called the Empyrean."

"Never heard of it. How's the barber though? Pretty good?"

Bob swallowed the last of his coffee. "Only been there once so far, but Diane is pretty good."

"You got a woman as your regular barber? Good Lord!" Walter adjusted his coffee cup so that it slid into the middle circle of the saucer. "Well, I just don't believe in those things." Walter lifted his hat and scratched his bald head. "I don't go to a barber anymore, but when I did it was Tony's down the street. And, you know, that's where you had a chance to vent a little — you know, get stuff off your chest, complain about the mayor, defend the Yankees, all that stuff." He dropped the hat back on his head. "Jeepers, Bob, I just don't know. To be honest, I have never known a woman barber."

Bob put his arm around Walter and gave him a squeeze, "Actually, Walter, they're called stylists now, not barbers. Barbers are out."

Walter lifted his hat into the air with his left hand and wiped his forehead with his right. "Geez, I don't know. Maybe I'm getting too old, but sometimes I think things have gone too far. Well, I better head home." He groaned a bit as he lifted himself up from the chair. "Just like my old man — always groaned when he got up from his chair. Now I know. Good luck, with — what did you call her, your stylist?"

· · · · ·

Bob hugged the inside lane of the Latham Traffic Circle and then just managed to cut in front of a red Corvette and head north on Route 9. He turned right on Cobbler

Lane and immediately the bright lights of the Empyre-an announced, "You have arrived." The last time he had been here was six weeks ago and much earlier in the day. He liked Diane, but for the heck of it he couldn't remem-ber her last name. Didn't really matter though — he had enough cash, so a check and that awkwardness wasn't an issue. What mattered was that she had given him a good haircut. He knew she was pretty good because a number of people at State Ed had complimented him on the sharp look. Rita was right — she'd been telling him for some time, "Diane cuts men's hair too — you should try her. Get a little style." Once Diane had seen his tired, dishev-eled look she immediately suggested a cool business cut with a natural side part. She pointed out that the cut was ideal for men over six feet tall, and at 6' 2" Bob was there. She seemed like someone he could trust, and he gave her the thumbs-up.

As he pulled into the jammed parking lot, all he could see were BMWs, Vettes, and an assortment of SUVs. No slots open. He pulled ahead and saw a space along the wall of the building ... maybe, could he do it, yes, and slipped his Ford into the slot, almost hidden from view.

As he approached the entrance, Bob felt the steps vi-brating to the beat of Huey Lewis and the News' "The Heart of Rock and Roll" — and then doors triggered by an electric eye opened for him — he felt kingly. A reception-ist, dressed in a leopard-patterned blouse, dark pants, and knee high boots, strolled past him and stopped, turning in his direction. Her hair was evenly divided — on the right side, a frenzied dance; on the left, combed straight down with what appeared to be the letter D cut into the scalp. She held an emory board in her right hand. "You have an appointment with?"

"Diane at 7:30," Bob felt dizzy from the sweet, penetrating fragrances, much stronger than he recalled from his last visit. Maybe the afternoons weren't so charged, he mused.

"She'll be with you in a few," said the receptionist, gesturing with her emory board at the chairs arranged along the separating partition.

Before sitting, Bob glanced back at the series of receding cubicles. Diane's was the third one back, and he could see her blow-drying someone's brilliant red hair. Bob breathed a sigh of relief. He was next.

Across from Bob and down two seats, two teen-aged girls dressed in jeans and almost matching low-cut blouses giggled behind magazines they held in front of their faces. He heard a loud pop and then another — bubble gum! He wished he had ear plugs. He grabbed the stack of magazines next to him and started flipping through them — *Cosmopolitan* — "How to Score Big at the Office Party," *People, Us, Shape, Hollywood Style, Vogue,* and *Ultra.* He picked out *Shape* and scanned the articles, "How to Fight Insidious Fat," "Six Yoga Moves That Will Start Your Day Right," "Pizza That Rocks Your Body," and "Confession of a Closet Snacker." He was flipping to the yoga article when the doors opened and a small, red-faced man dressed in a grey sweat-suit entered, gesticulating to the receptionist who had looked up suddenly from doing her nails. "Toots," he said running his hand through his thick head of hair, "Oh my God — I just don't believe that dinner with mother took that long. Toots, listen, is Sam still waiting for me?"

"Yes, Freddie," she said, "he is so set for you."

And Freddie disappeared behind the partition.

Bob closed his magazine. He couldn't concentrate — the thick smells, music amped up too high for him, and the growing din from behind the partition. He gripped the metal arms of his chair. He noticed a slight movement to his right, and he saw that the receptionist had dropped her emory board and bent down to pick it up. Now she was looking directly at him. He looked away and then back again — and she was still looking at him.

One of the girls had dropped her magazine on the stack and then noticed *People* with Prince on the cover. She picked it up, "Prince is so cool. He has got to be the coolest person! The other girl appeared from behind her magazine with a huge bubble in front of her face — POP. "See," the first one continued, "Michael wanted Prince to dance with him in 'Bad,' but Prince said, 'I don't need it, Michael. Really, I don't.' Love Prince, he is one major freak."

Her girlfriend was now staring at her reflection in the mirror to Bob's left and snapping her gum. "Um, yeah, but do you think I should have it blown tonight or just leave it natural?"

"Oh God, natural. Natural!"

Then the two heads disappeared behind the magazines again.

"Bobby?"

Bob turned back to his right and saw Diane's head floating above the partition. "Bobby, can you give me another ten? I am so sorry, but my client's got a really big party tonight — and she needs a few extra special touches."

"Sure, you're good, Diane." Diane must trigger good vibes, he thought, because "I Heard It Through the Grapevine" was now filling the Empyrean. He sat back and then heard hysterical laughter coming from the two magazine heads. Wonder what Walter would think if he saw this place, Bobby thought. He would never set foot in the door, he was sure. In many ways, Walter reminded him of his own father. His Dad had been his sole barber for the first ten years of his life.

In the kitchen, his father would place a bathroom towel on Bob's shoulders and with his left hand on top of Bob's head start upwards from the base of his neck with small hand clippers. Bob loved the feel of the cool grooves at the base of the clippers on his neck. When his father was done with the clipping, he would comb Bob's hair down onto his forehead, often over his eyes and with scissors resting just above the right eyebrow, he would cut straight across.

In fifth grade, Bob had fallen in love with Ellen. He started paying careful attention to his own looks. And so one Sunday afternoon, when his parents were out visiting friends at the other end of the village, Bob found his father's clippers on the top shelf in the kitchen, next to the bottle of Scotch. He slipped up to the bedroom to give himself a "really good" haircut.

Needless to say, the haircut was a disaster, and so one week later his father had taken him to Art's Barbershop in Center Brunswick to repair the damages and to get his first professional haircut. Waiting for Art, Bob enjoyed the low hum of the radio while looking at the *Montgomery Ward's Catalogue, Outdoor Life* and *Field and Stream.* Sitting in Art's barber's chair, he recalled the gentle buzzing on his neck from the electric clippers. Art's scissor and comb work, swift and precise, seemed like nimble dancers on the top of his head. To finish up, Art would pour some witch hazel on his hands and then place his hands on the back of Bob's neck rubbing the liquid in, its intoxicating fragrance sending Bob into a different zone. For the final touch, and it was a beaut, Art would attach a hand massager to his right hand and then starting with the back of Bob's neck, he would extend the massaging hand out over one shoulder, then the other, and back to the neck for another minute. Once Bob actually drifted off, and Art had to say, "All done, Bobby."

Bob looked at his watch — 7:40. He really didn't mind waiting. After all, he had no place to go except home, and Rita was away. And the haircut, well, it was pretty important. He remembered the day David, his unit manager, had said, "Bob, we've got to work on your image. You have to deal with people regularly, and you're too unkempt — people don't take you seriously. Maybe a haircut by a professional might help — nothing against your barber, but you really need to kick up your look, your style, you need some sharpness." And when he had told Rita, she had said, "Bob, I know you are not a salon type of guy, but Diane is excellent. She'll give you such a cool style that Dave will flip over it, and then you will be even more successful."

"Bobby, you're on," Diane called out and motioned for him to follow.

Bob got up and turned to follow her. In her light green pants and her pink blouse, Diane, who was some distance ahead of him, walked with confidence and grace. No question, she was a steadying force and guide in this glittering world. She turned a sharp left and disappeared as "Pour Some Sugar on Me" enveloped the room. A burst of laughter. He looked over to see someone with a head that looked like a ball of huge bandages settle into a chair. An orange and magenta creature slipped by — her hair exploding with enormous rollers, a lit cigarette dangling from her lip. Dizziness, and then he turned and saw Diane standing at the side of the sink. She was smiling.

"Well, Bobby, you're on your own for few days. Rita told me about the Conference and that I should take good care of you."

He laughed and then he sat in the chair as she placed a black canvas-like sheet over the front of him. "Just lean back, Yes, that's it."

He felt very relaxed as she adjusted the temperature of the water and then began to direct its stream into his hair. "I can't get over how busy it is tonight. Everyone seems to have a major party or big event to go to."

She now was lathering his scalp and then massaging it. He remembered how good it felt when Art would put that machine on his shoulders and neck, but this was a few notches above that.

"I got out of class at 4:00, drove right here, and the place was already jumping."

"You're going to school? Busy woman."

She had started to rinse his hair with the warm water. "Yes. God — I can't believe it. At the Valley. I'd really like to start my own hair business some day, but I need to do more, gain more confidence first."

"Uh huh,"

"I love school. Of course with my job here, I don't have a lot of free time." She finished with the rinsing and reached for a towel, and with one swift move, wrapped it around Bobby's head and secured it. "Follow me," she said.

· · · · ·

In her chair, Bobby watched Diane look at his hair. "Ok, so we'll keep the natural side part, do some light layering the way we did last time, and then blow dry it so you can just comb it easily or even run your fingers through it to give it that really natural look."

"Sounds good to me," he said. And then he watched her work, with a natural ease, almost as if her hands were floating. He could hear Bruce Springsteen's "Dancing in the Dark," and it almost seemed to him that Diane could probably cut someone's hair in the dark.

He didn't see anyone sit down, but then he saw a presence next to Diane in the mirror. The receptionist. She was seated a few feet to the right, behind him and facing a mirror on the opposite wall. He looked right at her. At first he thought she might be looking back, but when he concentrated he could see that she was studying herself and playing with her hair. He became transfixed by the movement of her fingers through her hair. She would take her fingers, run them gently down the right side of her face, just grazing her skin. Then just below the earlobe, she would gather strands of hair with her thumb, index and middle fingers and extend the hair out slowly into space, creating a graceful curve. She would then rub the strands with her fingers until one by one or in small groups, the strands broke free and fell back to her head and neck. Then she would do it all over again. Bob was transfixed.

Diane adjusted his head slightly. He wanted to ask her about the receptionist and why she was hanging out here rather than up front, but this seemed impertinent. He looked again. Did the receptionist notice him watching her?

"I'm taking an English course too," Diane said, as she clipped behind his ear. "God, how I hated English in high school, but this one is pretty good." Bob listened absent-mindedly as he studied the receptionist, who seemed entranced with herself. "We keep a journal and discuss stories in class. Last week we read a story by F. Scott Fitzgerald called 'Winter Dreams.' I really liked it, and the Professor said that if we liked it we should read *The Great Gatsby*. So I bought *Gatsby* a few days ago, and I'm already about half way through. It's a very sad book. Oh, and I'm 30, the same age as Nick, the narrator."

As Diane talked on about Gatsby and his parties, Bob continued studying the receptionist who was fixated on the right side of her head. He had begun to think of her as a permanent part of the mirror when someone shouted, "Cheryl, it's Marie." The receptionist slowly got up but kept her head tilted to the right, and maybe Bob imagined this, but as she emerged on the other side behind him, she seemed to be looking directly at him.

And then she was gone. "Diane, that woman behind us, Cheryl, I believe. She seems pretty spooky — all she did for twenty minutes was stare at herself in the mirror and play with her hair."

"Oh, Cheryl, yeah, she is strange," and then Diane leaned in close and whispered, "She's the daughter of the guy who owns this place. Receptionist work is part-time, and she seems pretty free to come and go when she feels like it. And that business of people staring at themselves here — that's pretty common. We even have a few stylists who stare at their own hair more than at the hair of their customers. Sammy, the gay guy down three chairs, calls these people mirror queens. He says the mirror becomes their kingdom, and they reign in it. Cheryl is here most nights, but then usually heads down to Flirtations."

"Flirtations?"

"Supposedly the hot spot — at the Marriott, you know the hotel on Wolf Road."

"Oh, I know the place. I worked there a few summers during college. I did some waiting on tables and some bell-hop work. No Flirtations though in those days."

"She likes it, says their band plays the latest stuff — U2, INXS, Dire Straits — groups like that. Well, look at you, you are done."

Bob looked at himself in the mirror. He looked thinner, a little more handsome, someone with a winning look. "You got the touch, Diane. Nice work. Still the same price?"

"Twenty-eight," she said.

Bob handed her two twenties — she was worth it. "Thanks, Diane, see you in a few weeks."

"Great, and don't forget to remind Rita of her appointment next Thursday. Diane set the money on the counter and removed *The Great Gatsby* from her pocketbook. "I got fifteen minutes before my next appointment — think I will read a few pages. Heading out for a beer or heading home?"

"Oh, I'm heading home. Pretty weary. Long day."

"Take care, and thanks, Bobby."

The receptionist was gone when he left, replaced by a short woman with purple-colored hair. As he slowly backed his car out, he thought he saw someone sitting in a blue Jag located behind him. He then put the car in drive and looked again at the Jag. It was Cheryl, and this time she was not looking in the mirror but right at him. "Hummmm," he wondered if it might be his hair cut that had her attention. He drove out of the lot slowly and gazed back at the Jag whose head lights were now on. When he reached Route 7, he turned right and headed west. He turned his radio from FM to AM and a pop station. It was Oldies Night and Gene Vincent's "Be-Bop-A-Lula" was playing. He started tapping on the steering wheel, "She's my baby," and then he saw the sign for the Northway south. He caught his image in the mirror — yes, he was looking good. He turned and headed south. He might just drive by the Marriott and see what was going on.

Geranium

Sister Agnes studied the three wrinkles in her habit. "Humph," she muttered and ran her fingers back and forth across the creases located just above her right knee. There was a time when there would have been no flaws in her habit, perfect, but with her arthritis gaining more and more ground, she had developed a bit of a laxity that had never been there. Her hands were now gnarled and her movements sometimes clumsy. She could also feel the encroachment of the arthritis in her joints, and sometimes the pain was severe. Still, she did all she could to keep up, and the rest of the Sisters would just have to accept her for what she was. "Where is Sister Irene?" she wondered. She looked at her watch. The wake began at three, and she wanted to get there a bit early, to avoid the crowd of course, and to be one of the first to pay her respects to Mr. Jackson. He would have smiled at that.

Mr. Jackson had always been kind of a whirling dervish — spinning, laughing, teasing — sometimes, he had pushed the envelope a bit too far, his little racy jokes — hmmmm — she smiled to herself, and always talking about those awful Yankees — how great they were, and forever that cigarette dangling from his lip. She would never admit it, but on a few occasions she had been so tempted to ask him for a cigarette. He probably would have roared and said something like, "Sister Agnes, I always knew you wanted one. Here you go."

How bold he had been at times, imagine telling her that she should really think seriously about giving up the habit — after all she was one of the last holdouts, along with Sister Florence. Sometimes he had been so exasperating. She recalled that winter day in her classroom when the heat had shut off inexplicably. Suddenly he had appeared in the doorway. And with the class at full attention, she had looked directly at him and said, "How do you expect me to teach *The Merchant of Venice* in a classroom as cold as this one?" His eyes suddenly flashed, "Well, Sister Agnes, you can teach dancing." And he was gone in a flash, and her class couldn't stifle their laughter.

She had found him outside the basement door, stretched out on the walkway, his left hand coiled over his heart and his right hand stretched out in the direction of a geranium, its roots on the cement, as if he had thrown it forward as he fell. Terrified, she had bent down and touched his forehead — so cold. "Mr. Jackson," she said, "please no, don't leave us." Once she had made the call, she had grabbed her afghan from the parlor, returned to the walkway, and then gently placed the afghan over him.

"Ready, Agnes?" Sister Irene stood in the doorway, in a yellow blazer, white blouse, and navy skirt.

"I'm coming," Sister Agnes said and slowly eased herself up and out of the rocking chair. Without looking, she could see Sister Irene shake her head. She also knew that Irene loved to show off her dark auburn hair. And when Agnes looked at Irene, she knew what was missing, the Cross of the Order.

"This shouldn't take long, should it?" Irene had asked once she was driving. Agnes was simply letting the local shops roll by her eyes — Duncan Donuts, Tire Warehouse, McDonald's, Tony's Used Cars — God, when had all this blight taken over — she wondered before answering, "I shouldn't think so." Sister Agnes had also become aware of the faint smell of cigarette smoke. Was Irene smoking? Having left the nun's habit some time ago, had she started another habit?

. . . . .

"Olive never felt very comfortable with the nuns," Sister Irene said as they walked to the car after paying their respects.

"Really," Sister Agnes said opening the car door. "Why do you say that?"

Sitting in the driver's seat with the key in her hand, Sister Irene said, "I'm not sure I'd be too thrilled if my husband worked as a janitor in a school run by a house full of celibate women."

"Now, what in God's name are you saying?" Sister Agnes remembered a line her mother used to say, "Sometimes some people just need a good, hard slap." Sister Agnes wanted so much to reach over and slap that smug little face.

"I don't recall seeing that woman at any of our staff parties over the last three years. The other spouses showed up."

"Well," Agnes was seething, "I can't think of one thing he ever did to make her jealous."

. . . . .

Olive, wearing a maroon pants suit, had taken Sister Agnes' hand very briefly and then turned to her right towards a tall young woman dressed in a dark green jacket, a beige blouse, and a black skirt. "Sister, you remember Marguerite?"

"Goodness gracious, Marguerite," said Sister Agnes and she took and held Marguerite's hand with both of hers, "how good to see you. It's been some time."

"Hi, Sister," Marguerite said and leaned in for a hug.

"I'm so sorry about your father, Marguerite, so sudden and so unexpected. I am sure God has a special place for him."

"Thank you, Sister," Marguerite said, tears welling in her eyes. Her mother's hand appeared on her daughter's right shoulder.

Sister Agnes stared into Marguerite's eyes. "What a wonderful little helper you were for your father, Marguerite, when our school was getting started. I still remember you running up and down the hall when your father was fixing a leak in one of the showers. "This is really neat," you said, "like my own hotel." And I still remember that you asked me if someday you could come and live with us." Marguerite was smiling.

Someone else had arrived to pay her respects, and Olive had interjected, "Thank you for coming, Sister," and she gently pulled her daughter back to her side.

· · · · ·

Sister Irene was standing by the door and looked at Sister Agnes with a degree of impatience, as if to say, "Are you done?" In the quiet of the car, except for Sister Irene's rapid tapping on the top of the steering wheel, Sister Agnes stared at the highway ahead. She was ready to be back in her rocking chair in the convent.

The car slowed suddenly, and Sister Irene said, "I need to make a quick stop at CVS. I have a few things to pick up. You don't mind waiting, do you, Sister?'

Sister Agnes watched the yellow blazer disappear behind the gray fortress-like wall of the pharmacy. She tried to stretch her legs a bit and felt the tightness of the arthritis in her knees and ankles. He was gone for good, she thought. She was so used to his coming and going for nearly twenty years, but this time he was gone for good.

Her head slipped back against the seat rest, and she closed her eyes. On the sidewalk he had been reaching for that single geranium, a few inches ahead on the cement. Where was he going to plant it? Had he planted others she wasn't aware of? That geranium was now in the window of her room in a small pot. She turned her head slightly to the right — oh, the sun was so warm. The black habit made it warmer, of course, but she didn't mind. The black still felt right — it was a witness. "Oh, Mr. Jackson," she sighed, "Mr. Jackson."

Black — that's what they all wore the day they arrived at the Academy over 22 years ago. Six Sisters in the big Buick station wagon that cool Saturday morning in July. And there stood Mr. Jackson on the patio with a large thermos of coffee, styrofoam cups, and a box of donuts, everything from jelly to cinnamon. "Welcome. Good Sisters, to Schenectady, New York, the city that lights the world." Ahhhh, she still remembered how tasty those donuts had been — she even had two of the jellies, and the coffee was perfect, even in the styrofoam cups.

The Sisters knew that the Diocese had assigned a custodian and his home would be a house on the property of the school. It would be ideal for emergencies and for simple convenience. Agnes had been assigned the task of keeping Mr. Jackson informed of anything in the house that needed attention. And that was how they became friends in spite of the fact that he was forever saying, "That Sister Agnes can find more jobs for me to do than Carter has liver pills."

He had just replaced a pane of glass in the community room one day as Sister Agnes entered holding the *New York Times*. "Hey, Sister, I've got some news for ya. Ollie is pregnant."

"Congratulations," she had said, though she wasn't sure that was the right word.

"Thank you, Sister," he said and smiled. "You keep me so busy over here it's a wonder I had time." He must have sensed her uneasiness. "Just teasing you, Sister. But I'll tell you, Ollie is already talking about names. Girls' names. She has no doubt that the baby is a girl." He pulled out a pack of cigarettes, "Mind if I light one up?"

"Please, go ahead," she said. She was used to the aroma of his cigarettes. She opened the drawer of a small table next to the sofa and reached for an ashtray the Sisters kept for visitors.

He took the ash tray from her and held it in his left hand as he inhaled deeply.

"What names has she thought of?" Sister asked.

"Well, she already has three names — listen to these: Roberta, Louise, and I really don't like this one — Eleanor, after some great aunt or something. You got any better suggestions?" He took another drag.

"Well, Mr. Jackson, I like your wife's second choice — I have a good friend named Louise, but I would like to add one more name to her list. What do you think of the name Marguerite?"

"Marguerite?"

"Yes," she looked at him for a moment and then smiled. "Of course, I wouldn't want to cause any friction between you and Olive."

"God, no. You'll never have to worry about that with Ollie. Hum, Marguerite, that does have kind of a nice ring to it."

· · · · ·

The yellow blazer was moving rapidly toward the car and Sister Irene's auburn hair seemed to be on fire. Opening the back door, Sister Irene placed the bag of items from the drugstore on the floor of the car. Getting in the car, she glanced at Sister Agnes, "Having a little snooze?"

"No, just resting my eyes."

Sister Irene eased out of the lot and was back on State Street. She cleared her throat, "Flo and Ceil will probably join you for dinner tonight. Maura can fix you some salad, and you three can finish the rest of the chicken."

Sister Agnes couldn't resist, "You will be with us, correct?"

"No."

"Another meeting?"

"Yes, I am talking with Bob about a possible position next year."

They were turning up Marriott toward the school. "You're not going to teach?"

Sister Agnes had not looked at Sister Irene, but she felt Irene's cold stare. "I am considering my options," Sister Irene said slowly.

. . . . .

Arriving five years after the academy had opened, Sister Irene had worn the full habit for two years and then had shifted with a few other nuns to the modified habit and even a simple head veil. Sister Agnes was, for the most part, comfortable with this change. Though the new habit was a dramatic shift from the full habit the Sisters had worn for over forty years, she felt that some compromise was probably necessary for the younger nuns, and the habit the order had settled on was simple, modest, and appropriate. In her classroom, Sister Irene was a crackerjack as a teacher of

English. Solidly grounded in the classics and in the fundamentals of writing, Sister Irene worked her students hard, and they seemed to like being in the presence of a Sister who was witty and "with it."

There had been a couple of classroom text issues along the way that caused some concern for Sister Agnes, one about a story Irene had done with her seniors.

The story was "In the Region of Ice," and Sister Agnes had gotten a copy and read it. The darkness and ambiguity of the story plus the stunning fact that the central character in the story was a nun with the name Sister Irene troubled Sister Agnes. One night after dinner, she asked Irene about the story.

"Ahhhh yes, I find Oates really hits home on what it feels like to be unable to connect with others. I think some of the students really locked into the story."

"But the ending is so dark," Sister Agnes said.

"True, but sometimes life can be pretty dark. It's pretty clear that Allen was in his own world, bound in by ice."

"Sister Irene — I mean the one in the story," Sister Agnes said, "did try to reach out, in her own way."

Sister Irene finished the water that was left in her glass. "She did, but in a way she too was trapped."

"Why do you say that?"

"She wanted to do more, but she was unable, and in the end she really rejected him, even though he was attacking her and in a desperate state. She was unable to reach him."

"I am not sure anyone could have," Sister Agnes said.

And then there had been *Othello*. When she taught the seniors, Sister Agnes had stressed the idea of the tragic flaw, and she felt that it was pretty obvious that Othello's flaw was jealousy. "But, Sister Agnes, that's simply too narrow a view," said Sister Irene, one afternoon in the community room. "I mean, look at the play for a second — how can you avoid dealing with the issue of race, the way Iago speaks of Othello in the first scene, and it never ceases. And what about the role and position of women in this text. I mean talk about the lack of power and voice."

Sister Agnes had felt lectured to. "Just be careful, Sister Irene. Don't get too carried away with some of these modern notions."

"They are there, Sister Agnes. I refuse to wear a blindfold."

· · · · ·

The community had adjusted reasonably well to the option of wearing the modified habit, the younger Sisters all opting for it, the older nuns struggling to leave the old habit, and the middle-aged nuns testing out a range of modifications. Understanding and acceptance, however, was not the case when the decision came from the office of Superior General to allow the Sisters the option of choosing a layperson's attire. It had been Sister Agnes' thinking from the beginning that the more you moved away from the habit, the more likely you were moving away from your calling. It was in her mind like those who sat in the last few rows at Church, then stood in the back, and eventually were gone.

And so here we were, she reflected, in yellow blazers, navy skirts, and no visible sign of a religious commitment. "Sister Agnes," Sister Irene had said, "if people are going to judge your spiritual commitment by the clothes you wear, then they are pretty shallow." Sister Agnes would simply say, "We need visible witnesses."

Three Sisters had left the house the previous year, two to do other ministries, one for a leave of discernment. Sister

Agnes knew that teaching no longer seemed to be flowing in their veins, but that had been their mission, their declared commitment. And Mr. Jackson had observed it all.

One day she had been reading *them,* a novel by Joyce Carol Oates that Sister Irene had left in her mailbox, when Mr. Jackson slipped in and plopped down on the sofa of the community room before she realized he was there.

"You love your books, don't you, Sister, didn't even see me come in."

Sister Agnes smiled and set the book on the coffee table. She was actually glad to see someone in the real world, for the world of Maureen Wendall, the central character, was pretty harsh.

"Mr. Jackson, it's good to see you. Could I get you a cup of tea?"

"No, Sister, I just need a short break. I got a few projects going. Just finished taking six chairs out of Sister Lucy's classroom. She says she doesn't need them and that she can make good use of the space. That leaves only 19 chairs in her room. Are we losing students, Sister?"

"I think we are down to about 380 students."

"How low can we go before we are in trouble?"

"If we get to 300, that's an issue," said Sister Agnes, sitting more upright in her chair.

Mr. Jackson pulled a pack of cigarettes out of his shirt pocket. "Danger of closing?"

"I am afraid of that," she said.

"I wonder if the Diocese would let me make an offer on the house if the school closed."

"Goodness yes. I am sure they would."

Mr. Jackson had removed a cigarette and was tapping it on the arm of the sofa. "What would you do, Sister, if the school closed."

"Probably go to one of our other schools. Continue to teach, I am sure. And you, Mr. Jackson?"

"Well, Marguerite is a senior now. Once she is out of high school, we won't have to worry too much. She will find something. I can probably find a janitor's job some place in the city. Really hate to see this place close though. Some good years here." He looked at her and smiled, "Well," he paused to exhale, "let's not worry too much more today."

· · · · ·

"I wish you had told me you were going over to the wake this afternoon, Sister Agnes." Sister Florence stared at Sister Agnes and pushed her glasses back up the bridge of her nose.

"I am sorry, Sister Florence. I did think that the car would be available for you and Sister Cecilia."

Sister Cecilia glanced up from her plate, emitted a "hundt" sound, and set her fork down. She reached into her habit and pulled out a deck of cards, which she placed directly in front of her plate.

Sister Florence looked at the cards for a second and then began to cut a small breast of chicken into tiny portions. "Some people around here need to start thinking of others."

Sister Agnes felt her blood starting to rise, "Are you suggesting, Sister, that I intended to leave you and Sister Cecilia here?"

"I am not blaming anyone, Sister, but I do remember a time when Sisters who wanted to go out for the evening would check with the rest of the community to see if anyone would be inconvenienced." She had speared a tiny piece of chicken and held it in front of her face inspecting it.

"Pass the pepper, Sister," said Sister Cecilia, tapping the top of the deck of cards with her index finger.

Agnes reached for the pepper and passed it to Cecilia, but her eyes were focused on Florence as she very slowly directed the fork with the morsel of chicken into her mouth.

Florence wiped her mouth deliberately with her napkin and then said, "Where did the good little Sister Irene go this evening?"

Sister Agnes was guessing, "I believe it had something to do with organizing the arts festival at the Bridge Center and then talking to Father Bob about an issue."

"Cards anyone? I mean tea anyone?" Cecilia had risen from the table.

"Yes, please, a cup of tea," said Agnes.

"No thank you, Sister Cecilia," Florence said and then leaned in toward Agnes, "Frankly, Agnes, I don't like the way Irene is behaving. I mean, this is not a hotel where you can come and go as you please."

Agnes watched the veins filling in Florence's forehead. "Now look, Florence."

"Don't you 'Now look, Florence me,' Agnes. I am sick and tired of her behavior. This is a community, for God's sakes!"

"Florence," Agnes reached across the table and placed her hand down on Florence's left hand, which held her napkin tightly. "You need to calm down, please."

"Is there something wrong, Sisters?" Cecilia stood in the doorway holding a teapot in her right hand.

"No, we're fine," said Agnes as she lifted her hand from Florence's.

"Well, then, since we are 'trapped' here for the evening, would you two dear friends consider a delightful game of Hearts?"

"If Florence will join us, I would be happy to play Hearts," Agnes said.

. . . . .

In her room, Sister Agnes sat in her chair staring out at the back parking lot, the two street lights casting a pale yellow blanket over the pavement. She had not encouraged Florence and Cecilia to do evening prayer after their few rounds of Hearts. She held her evening Office on her lap, and she looked down at a well-worn card that Mother St. Anne had given her on the day of her final vows. On the back the words, "To Sister Agnes, may you live as a true daughter of Mother Marguerite." And on the front was a simple sketch of a young woman kneeling and below her the words, "My being proclaims your greatness, and my spirit finds joy in you, O God, my Savior. For you have looked upon me, your servant, in my lowliness."

She saw lights at the entranceway to the parking lot, and she watched the car as it pulled into the reserved spot right in front of the convent. Sister Irene got out and walked quickly toward the door and disappeared out of sight.

Sister Agnes felt the weight of the day. She gazed to her right at the geranium. "Good night, Mr. Jackson," she said and turned toward her bed.

. . . . .

On the kitchen table was an envelope with the words "To My Sisters" on the front. Sister Agnes opened the envelope and removed the short note.

Dear Sisters,

I would have preferred speaking with each one of you about my decision, but time is precious and this note must suffice for now. I have gathered my essential belongings, and I am already on the train to Staten Island to spend a few days with my uncle who, as you know, recently suffered a heart attack. Then in answer to what I believe is the Spirit's Call in my life, I have, with the Council's permission, accepted a position as a staff member of St. Anthony's Renewal Center. This position is for me an answer to prayer and a long-awaited opportunity for ministry to which I feel called. As in most life-changing decisions, there is pain involved in leaving our school.

Please pray for me as I will continue to pray for you.

Irene

Sister Agnes left the envelope on the table and slowly returned to her room. Today was Mr. Jackson's Funeral. "She couldn't even wait for that," she mused. She went to the window and opened it. Sitting down, she felt the morning breeze and inhaled the scent of the geranium. She would sit for a bit longer and then gather the Sisters in the house and set out for Mr. Jackson's funeral Mass.

The Otter Creek Eel

From her wheelchair on her son's newly constructed deck, Marian could see it all, all that mattered: her three sons, one on a riding lawn mower and two behind power mowers, creating a lawn in the field that rolled down to the source of so much of her childhood happiness, Otter Creek, to her eyes now like a shimmering silver ribbon.

In the breeze millions of specks of grass danced wildly to the cutting blades — Daniel and John striding behind power mowers as they created rectangular patterns in front of the house and David, her oldest, near the creek looping and twisting in circular patterns around an ancient fallen tree and a clump of blackberry bushes.

When the water was frozen over in winters past, Marian's five brothers, much to their mother's chagrin, would ride down the slope and right onto and across the frozen water. Once John, the oldest, was crossing the water and the ice gave way and he sank into the icy stream. She remembered the boys helping him out and laughing on the way up the hill to the house, but when he came into the kitchen, he was nearly frozen. Marian used to watch her brothers from the front window of the old homestead, its remaining foundation only fifty yards from where she now sat, as her brothers soared down the hill through snow tunnels they had created, some as long as 20 feet, and emerge, even faster heading for the creek at the bottom. Once both she and her mother roared when two of the boys went down the hill together, Bill lying on top of Larry, and miscalculated the height of the tunnel.

Fearful of too much sun, Marian released the brake on her wheelchair and moved into the shadow created by the large pine tree which fronted the left side of the house. Daniel's wife Ellen and John's girlfriend Marie both lay dozing in the sun on the far side of the deck. Marian felt comfortable with Ellen and her easy laugh, but Marie was still kind of a stranger, often moody and very opinionated. "I am really a city person," she announced shortly after arriving.

David was climbing the steep bank of the road that passed over the creek, a bridge formed by loads of gravel dumped around a huge steel pipe through which the water ran. She gripped the arms of her wheelchair as David's mower seemed to tip precariously. Though she had watched her husband, now dead seven years, mow those same banks without an accident, the action always made her tense. With the exception of superficial cuts and wounds natural to anyone who worked the land, Martin had never suffered a serious injury. It was a nagging ache in the stomach which he had complained about. She had suggested the doctor, but Martin didn't think kindly of doctors. And then, though it didn't seem possible in such a strong and robust man, it was too late. David disappeared on the far side of the bridge. She leaned forward and squinted, breathing a sigh of relief when he emerged from behind the large oak tree.

When she sat facing north on the old wooden bridge as a child, Marian used to drop daisies into the water and watch them disappear underneath. Once her mother shouted at her from the house, "Be careful or you'll fall in." About fifty yards north of the bridge in the middle of the creek sat

Grandpa, a huge rock that from a distance looked to her like the head of an old man, large enough for her to sit on. She was pretty sure that her mother never knew that her daughter once or twice a week in good weather would wade to the rock, holding her skirt up high. She would then climb onto the rock, nestle in comfortably, and chat with Grandpa about her brothers, the farm, her father — always so distant, and most of all her mother. When she leaned forward and looked into the water, she could see her own face distorted by the ripples, but when the creek was really slow, she could see hundreds of minnows. Once, while she was entranced by the dazzling playfulness of a butterfly along the shore, she saw the grass move below it, and a long black creature slid into the water. Her heart stopped, but then she remembered her mother's words a few weeks earlier when the two of them were crossing the bridge. Her mother had stopped and stared toward the water, and when Marian looked in the same direction, there was a dark movement in the water. Her mother's hand had wrapped around her shoulder, "An eel, Marian, don't worry. They're harmless." And now to Grandpa, Marian said, "Grandpa, don't worry, it must be an eel. They are harmless." She continued to say, "Don't worry, Grandpa" until she had waded with some fear back to shore.

Farther up the stream, and strictly off-limits to her — Mother's rule — was the Deep Hole. Camouflaged by the overhang of trees, the creek had over time formed a natural pool. "Tell me about the pool," Marian had said one day to Eddie, her favorite brother.

"Well, Marian, it's not that wide — maybe 25 feet, but it's pretty deep. I mean I touched the bottom one day, and when I came back up, I was almost out of breath."

Marian wanted to go so bad and see the Deep Hole, but her mother forbid it.

"Marian, no! That place is for your brothers. It wouldn't be right for you to be there."

Marian suspected that the fact that her brothers always returned in dry clothes was a clue as to why her mother didn't want her there. She was sure the boys swam without any clothes.

And so, until long after she was married and had returned to the farm for a visit, she had not gone near the Deep Hole.

"Mam, such a nice tree?" Marian looked up at Ellen, who smelled of coconut, her eyes like blue-grey pebbles in her bronzed face. Marian adjusted her hearing aid and then reached for Ellen's arm. "What did you ask me?"

"Marian, would you like some iced tea?"

"No, not now, thank you." As she held Ellen's arm, she could hear the silence. "What happened to the boys? Did they stop?"

Ellen stepped back and looked down towards the creek. "Oh, there they are, sitting on the bank. Smoking those awful cigars of David's. I wish he wouldn't break those out."

"Now, Ellen, no need for concern. It's good for the boys to be together."

Ellen sighed and stepped back, letting Marian's hand slide off her arm. She turned and entered the kitchen. Marie was now lighting a cigarette. Funny, Marian thought, women never looked quite proper and dignified when smoking. She watched Marie exhale and then lean back into the lounge chair. Marian leaned forward and peered down to where she could just see the boys. Martin had smoked cigars for nearly forty years. She had grown accustomed to the aroma, which almost seemed like a natural extension of Martin. She remembered, however, how suddenly he had stopped after a growth on his lip failed to heal. He hadn't said much, but the dark, mole-like growth on his lip must have terrified him. And that year, he seemed to be actually eager, on their annual pilgrimage to shrines, to enter the Basilica of St. Anne-de-Beaupre in Quebec and kneel and pray and put holy water on his lip. In time, the growth faded and disappeared, and Marian's words about visiting shrines each spring took on more significance for Martin. Marian never saw him take another cigar.

Ripples of laughter from the creek reached her, echoing laughter from years ago. She remembered ascending the hill behind their home and following a rivulet whose source was a spring at the very back of their property. When she reached the spring, which flowed between a small cluster of rocks and then formed a small pool before it began its journey downward, she would squat down and with both hands held together, she would dip them into the water, draw them out and drink deeply. Then she would rub water over her eyes, copying her mother's habit of always blessing herself and then touching her eyes with holy water on the way in and out of church. Marian never questioned her mother, but she herself secretly believed that her own miraculous spring water on the hill was one of the reasons for her longevity. She was the lone survivor. John, the oldest, killed in France in World War I; Paul, a massive heart attack; Larry, emphysema; Bill and her favorite Eddie, both of cancer.

The boys had erupted in shouts. "There! Get it, David!' John was pointing at a spot along the bank. Daniel ran to a fallen tree and snapped off a dry branch. "Here," he shouted and threw the branch to David who caught it, turned, and beat at something in the high grass. "Oh, crap!" David shouted. And then there was silence.

"What in God's name are they doing now? asked Ellen who had just emerged from the house. Marie had sat up and was staring down at the stream.

"I can't tell from here," said Marian, "but it was most likely an eel."

"An eel? Up here?"

"Oh yes. I have to remind the boys that they shouldn't hurt eels, unless they need them for food. Do you remember, Ellen, the great Yankee, Lou Gehrig?"

"I think so. He played with Babe Ruth."

"Yes. When he was a boy, Lou and his father used to hunt eels — the family was very poor — for food. They used to hunt for them at night too."

"I really don't think it was an eel," said Marie, who was now standing. "It was probably a snake.'

Marian felt herself stiffen. "No, Marie. I don't think so. I am sure it was an eel. I have seen them before in this creek. Yes, they are definitely down there. But they're harmless, you know."

Her sons were now walking toward the house, laughing and replaying their little drama. For just a second, she saw her brothers returning from the Deep Hole — Bill and Paul always lagged behind and would be coming along soon. Laughter again. But these were her sons. She released the brake on her wheelchair and moved out of the shade. She had better remind them about the eels. It was important that they know.

Spikes

"Damnnnnnnnnnnnn," Vito said as Dan's ball continued to rise and finally disappear over a knoll in the center of the fairway.

"Hey, Dan-boy, sure this is your first game of the year?"

"Yes, Joey," Dan said as he knelt to tie the lace of his sneaker. "It's just a matter of youth starting to assert itself." Walking off the tee, he gazed out toward the knoll. "There's no pond behind the knoll, is there?"

"Let's hope so, for our sake," Vito said as he jumped into his cart, grabbed his can of Diet Coke, and shouted "Avanti" to Joe who was driving.

Roger was sitting in the passenger seat totaling the score. Dan got in, tapped the brake pedal, and then hit the accelerator. The cart lurched forward, "How we doing so far?"

Roger reached down to retrieve the pencil that had flown out of his hand. "After four holes, we are kicking some serious butt. Roger flipped the card and the pencil into the open compartment. 'Nice drive, but we have to keep playing well. I got this feeling that for the first time in eight long years, you and I, Dan, are going to do it." Roger removed his red golf hat and ran his fingers through his thinning hair. "Hot as a two dollar pistol out — you got any of that lotion available, you know, that number eighty that you use."

Dan took his foot off the accelerator and the cart eased to a stop. "Yeah, got some in my bag. I'll grab it while you take your shot. What are you going with, your five wood?"

Roger studied his bag of clubs, "Hummmm, maybe I'll try the old two iron." He pulled out the two and looked across the fairway, "Where the hell are those guys?"

Holding the lotion in his hand, Dan stared in the direction of the grove of pine trees on the right side of the fairway. A ball flew out from behind a tree. "My guess is that ball was thrown out, not hit," he said.

"Thrown, obviously," Roger said. "The question is how many swings were taken before the throw." Roger approached his ball and elevated it slightly with his two iron.

"You're out and clear," shouted Joe, who had just emerged from the pine trees. Joe's wardrobe of a bright canary-colored golf shirt and white baggy shorts did not buttress Joe's contention that he had recently lost ten pounds. Vito now appeared carrying two irons on his shoulder. In his khaki shorts and bright red golf shirt, he looked like a late-arriving warning flag.

Roger swung and sent a line drive that skipped twice before going over the knoll. "I should be up there near you," he said as he caught the lotion Dan had just flipped to him. "Son of a biscuit," Roger said, glancing back at the fifth hole, "those old buggers are really pressing us. We gotta get Vito and Joey to stop looking all day for their damn balls."

"Maybe we should let the foursome play through on the next hole," Dan said.

"Sure, what the hell, no rush, I guess. You know what, Dan-boy," Roger said as he rubbed some lotion on his neck, "this is great stuff being out together. Eight years now, isn't it? And you know what, it looks as if we are going to nail the old men for the first time. Crap, look at that shot."

Vito's long iron shot appeared as if it would make the green, but then seemed to lose thrust and fell short, disappearing into a front bunker. "I just love it — Vito in the sand!" Roger roared.

Dan was still smiling as he swung and caught the very top of his ball sending it about ten feet in front of them. Roger burst into laughter again. "I guess we better not get too cocky — the golf gods may turn on us." And for a moment Dan felt the spirit that had been so much a part of their togetherness, especially the first three years when they were all teaching at St. Martin's. He recalled how this had all started one Friday after school when they were relaxing with a couple of brews.

· · · · ·

"Listen, you guys, we've got to get together at least once this summer, maybe even an over-nighter or two," Vito said as he signaled the waitress for one more round. "I'm talking mucho serious now. Come on, what about it?"

Joe reached into the basket for the last of the popcorn. "Geez, I'm tied up for the month of July — the Brothers have a house in Denis Port. What about August some time?"

"I'm in for August," Vito said. "What about you, Danny Boy?"

Dan leaned up and butted his cigarette out in the ashtray. The effect of watching "Casablanca" until two in the morning was catching up with him. "Possibly," he muttered. Then he cleared his throat and said, "I do a little landscape work for my grandfather in the summer, but yeah, I can probably find a day or two."

"Solid," said Vito. "Roger, my man, can you get the old jockstrap out of the closet for a summer get together?"

"It's already on, and I am so ready," said Roger as the waitress arrived with the four beers.

"Thank you, Dear," said Vito, "you can give us the check now. Joey, you got this one?"

The others laughed as Joe let out a "Humph."

"One question," Roger said as he adjusted his glasses slightly with his left hand. "What will it be — Hiking? Fishing? Canoeing?"

"That's pretty rigorous stuff," Joe said. "I am not sure my body can handle it. What about some old-fashioned golf? I have played a bit of that."

"I prefer tennis," said Roger, "but I would give golf a whirl. I have to borrow my father-in-law's clubs though."

"Golf!" Vito said, "You kidding me, chasing a little white ball around. I don't know. I'd have to get a set of lessons before I tried that!"

"Vito, you'll love it, sitting back in the cart surveying the terrain. You'll feel like Patton. What about you, Dan?"

Dan took a sip of beer. "I'll need some clubs too. I could probably borrow some from Father Charles. I think I remember him saying that he still had his old set. I think the parents' club gave him a new set. And you know what, I just thought of something. My nephew is with Marriott, and I think he has been regional vp or something at a golf resort north of Atlantic City, for a few years now — Seaview or something like that. Maybe he could get us a deal — couple of nights — and we could get in a few rounds and also visit the casinos one night."

"Sounds great, Dan, " said Roger, "that would work."

Vito lifted his glass, "I think we got something cooking here. Gentlemen, here's to the St. Martin's Golf Classic, the first of many," and the four lifted their glasses of beer.

· · · · ·

"Old dudes can really whack the ball," Vito said as the last of the foursome they had waved through teed off on hole number six.

"Thank you, gentlemen," shouted the driver of the lead cart just before they pulled away.

"You betcha," said Vito, waving the golf ball that he held between his index finger and his middle finger.

They sat under a densely leafed oak tree on two benches that looked out on the fairway of the par five, sixth hole, a fairway that dipped and disappeared about 150 years out and then appeared again near the 350 yard marker. The two carts of the foursome had disappeared.

"What did you have, Vito, on the last hole, a nine?" asked Roger holding the score card in his hand?

"Horse's ass, a nine. I shot a solid seven."

"Really?" said Roger who looked quickly at Dan and winked. "Didn't you get a bit bogged down in the trap?"

"Yeah, but I was there in three."

"Joe? A seven?"

"I know — three bad shots or I would've had a par."

"All right. Dan and I both got sixes, so we got ourselves a game going here."

"Age will prevail," said Joe as he removed his hat and pulled up his shirt to wipe the sweat from his forehead, show-ing stretch marks that looked to Dan like a battered picket fence. "And the Vites and I still have the secret weapon."

Dan glanced at Roger and smiled and then leaned back into the cool slats of the bench. He let his head drop back, and he closed his eyes. For a second or two, all was silent and he felt a light breeze cross his face, like gently massag-ing finger tips.

"How much longer you going to stay at that place, Dan?" Vito was standing right in front of him. 'Nothing for nothing, but you ain't going to have much of a retirement with their freaking pension. You gotta get the hell outta there."

"Damn it," Dan said and drew a cigarette out of the pack in his shirt pocket.

"Dan, you know you could come over to Central High with me," Roger said as he dried his golf balls on the towel. "You'll love it. The money is great. And really, the kids aren't that much different. To be honest, some of them are a hell of a lot smarter than the St. Martin kids."

Dan took a drag on his cigarette, "I know, guys. I've heard it all before."

"Listen, Dan," Vito said as he started backing towards the tee with his driver on his shoulder. "You can carry this sacrifice shit just so far. I got the hell out. Roge made his move. Look, even Joey decided it was time to get out. And he left the Brothers, no less. Granted it took him a couple of years to get his ass off the pot, but from what I hear, he's one dam good guidance counselor now. Right, Joey?"

"Ahhh, I don't know. Kids are kids. None of them really know what's going on. They don't seem to have any morals."

"Come on, Joey, you got them into some good schools. Bobby's in U-Mass, Tom and Eddie at State, Ellen is at Union, and don't you have someone going to Princeton?"

"Maria Stills got in, but with 780 on the Boards and a 97 average, I didn't do much. Still they don't seem to have a moral center. No sense of sin at all."

"Dan," Vito said, while reaching down to place his tee, "I put fifteen years into St. Martin's, and I'm not bragging, but damn it, I will. I got four league championships to show for it. Believe me, I don't owe them a goddam thing. Until I got there, St. Martin's was shit. Should I hit or what?"

"Better wait until you see all of them," Joe said reaching for his driver.

"Yeah, you never know, I might get ahold of one." Vito took a step toward Dan who appeared to be gazing at the distant green. "Dan, you don't owe St. Martin's shit. I know you and Father Charles were goddam bosom buddies, but the old man is retired now. Father Doyle, I hear, is a real bastard."

"In the Sam Spade tradition?" Roger asked and then cackled.

"I'll Sam Spade you, you piece of crap," Vito said, pointing his driver at Roger.

"Vito," Dan had stood up and was heading toward his golf bag, "I'm working on it, okay? I'm doing some thinking." He pulled out his driver and moved toward Vito. "To be honest, I don't know where St. Martin's fits in at this point. Over the years, it's done a lot for me. But, one thing I do know though — I am not ready to lay it all out in front of you. If that's all right!"

"Your call, Dan," Vito said.

Roger stepped forward and put his hand on Dan's shoulder, "Vito, you can go ahead and hit. I can see all four geezers now."

"You're right. This is supposed to be a fun day, and Joey and I got to get serious about knocking you two dudes off. Get ready to shout "FORE" to those old codgers. I'm launching this baby!"

· · · · ·

"Listen," Roger said leaning into the center of the table, his right hand holding his onion-laden hot dog. I think I got an angle on getting head of department in one more year."

"You're shitting me," Vito said.

"No shit, Sherlock. Here's the deal. Mrs. Sherman, good woman — no question, but she's about 90 and has been telling everyone that she's ready to wrap it up. And I've been working on our hot shot principal with some stuff. He likes the fact that I've got a couple of articles published last year — not biggies, granted, but stuff out there — and the fact I have two master's. So, Dan, my friend, I am looking forward to being there with you at district coordinators' meetings."

Dan took a drag on his cigarette, exhaled, and then lifted his glass, "Here's to you, Roger. Seriously, all the best."

"Nice," said Joe, "Ok, back to serious business. Here's the total after nine big holes." He wiped his mouth with his napkin.

'Uh huh, then we'll give you our total," Roger said through a mouthful of onions.

"Vito — a fantastic 51!"

"Seriously?" Roger said.

"Let me finish, Roger," Joe said, holding up his hand. "Vito, 51, yours truly, 47. Dangerous Dan — a big 51, and Roger, we have you at an even 50. We are talking IBM accuracy, my boys."

Roger brushed a few stray onions off his score card. "I think I may be a little closer to the truth. Vito, we got you at 53. Joey, you have a 49. Dan, 49. And my score, ok, here we go. One more addition, yes, a 48."

'Ain't this a bitch!" Vito said as he leaned back in his chair and began to laugh. "I'll tell you though. I'd put my money on the scoring of an ex-Brother any day over some blind guy who is taking over a department after only two years in a school."

"Hey, Vito," Roger said, "you taught me the secrets of success."

"Screw you, Roger, I'll stick with my solid 51. Remember, losers buy, and we, my lad, don't intend to lose. Right, Brother Joseph?"

"Hey," Joe said glancing at the crowded table near them, "give me a break on the Brother reference."

"You got it, Joey," Vito said, rubbing his stomach with his right hand. "Hell of a cheeseburger, by the way, and that beer was cold, the way I like it. I have to grab a quick leak, and then that back nine is going to feel our presence." He stood up as Dan lit another cigarette, "Dan, you smoked about a pack this morning. When are you going to give those cancer sticks up?"

Dan inhaled and then blew the smoke in Vito's direction, "When I get my next hole in one."

· · · · ·

On the thirteenth hole, Dan sliced the ball into the rough, not too far from where Joe had hit his ball. He grabbed his 5 iron and headed toward the ball, "Go ahead, Roge, as long as there is no one pressing us, I'll walk this one out.'

"Wait up, " said Joe. "I'll join you. Gotta work that lunch off anyway."

Vito couldn't resist, "What about that large order of fries you had with your burger?"

"Where would an Irish guy be without his potatoes," said Joe as he reached for his 4 iron.

"In Little Italy," said Vito as he gunned the cart and roared away.

Walking across the fairway, Dan felt beads of sweat sliding down his back. The day was becoming hazy and very humid. He could hear Joe's labored breathing. As long as he had known Joe, there had been a weight problem, especially when Joe was a Brother. "Wouldn't mind having that breeze back," Dan said.

"Absolutely," Joe said. "Hey, Dan, I know Vito was kinda getting on your nerves back there. You know Vito. For better or worse, you always know where he stands. Listen, Dan, if I'm prying, let me know." Dan kept his head down as he walked. Joe continued. "You're the last of us at St. Martin's. And to be honest, you are a real enigma. Ten years ago, who would have guessed that I'd be gone before you. So many were making the move, and it all seemed to make sense. I mean Vito's got Carol and their two kids, you know. He needed more money and more security over the long haul — hang on a minute." Joe looked down at this ball, which had a decent lie, set himself for the shot, and swung, losing his balance a bit and slicing the ball sharply to the right, "Well, at least it's on the fairway." They kept walking toward Dan's ball. "Uhhh, where was I? And Roger, look at him. It was always clear that his stay would be temporary. We always thought of him as kind of a climber, not in an obnoxious way at all, but with you as department chair, where was he to go? And in a way, he is a bit of a buck artist. I know you're not interested in the money, Dan, but still, we can't figure out why the heck you stay at St. Martin's. What are we missing?"

They had reached Dan's ball, "Yeah, Joe, you're missing something, but I'm not exactly sure what it is. Let me hit this thing." Dan looked down at the ball, took his club back smoothly, and came back down, catching the ball just right, sending it straight toward the pin.

"Nice, shot," Joe said.

"Thanks. You're right, Joe. Sometimes I can't even figure my own action out. I feel as if I have made an impact at St. Martin's. You know, things mattered, and, by the grace of God, I had some success. I don't know. I don't know. But why you, Joe? You had roots, you had a community. You had people who seemed to care about you. What the hell happened to you, Joe? Wasn't community life worth it?"

The sun was bearing down, and Joe wiped his forehead with his right arm. "You know, the thing is, I guess, early, ahhh, I was in for almost 18 years, you know, but I'm just not sure what happened. Being a St. Martin's guy myself, I got to know a few of the Brothers there, and I guess after high school, I was really unsure of what I wanted to do. Brother Gene, remember him, good guy really, asked me if I wanted to become a Brother. And since I really didn't know, I decided I would try it. And I admit that once in the order, I liked it. I made some good friends there — Tommy Fritz, Bob McCardle, Ray Sherwood — you remember him, he was at St. Martin's three years before he was transferred. But then something happened — things began to fray — frankly some of the Brothers didn't seem to give a shit anymore — skipping Mass, evening prayer became a joke, and everyone wanted to do their own thing. I'd sit in my room nights and stare at the wall. I felt like that guy you mentioned in the story you used to teach — by Melville?"

"Bartleby."

"He's the one, something about, 'I prefer not to.'"

"That's it," Dan said, reaching for a cigarette.

Joe had reached his ball as Vito pulled up, "Your last shot was pretty pathetic, Joey."

"Caught some turf," Joe said. He pulled out his six iron, swung and hit a decent shot down the fairway.

"That's more like it," Vito said, "Ok, hop on."

"I think I'll walk with Dan."

"Dan, when the hell are you going to get some legitimate golf shoes?"

Dan who was bending down tying the lace on his right sneaker looked up at Vito. "These feel fine to me, Vito."

"Ok, you guys, sweat yourself to death — at least on the cart, you get a little breeze. See you on the green."

As Vito sped away, Joe continued. "So I made the move — the Brothers have this thing called exclaustration — a period in which you spend some time thinking about whether you want to leave the order or not. So I did a year of thinking while working odd jobs here and there, and then Vito called me to tell me there was a guidance position open at the Academy. That kinda did it. So I told the Brothers that I was ready to leave for permanent, and now — look at me I am getting Vito's football squad into some really good colleges."

Roger pulled up and said, "Want to grab a club?"

Dan looked at his ball and said sure, "Reaching for a nine iron. I'll grab my putter too."

"Sounds good," said Roger and waited a few seconds as Dan returned his club and took out the nine and the putter. "Hit it well," he said and drove off.

Dan swung and caught the ball just right, sending a high arching shot that landed on the right side of the green and rolled to the edge.

"Good shot," Joe said, as they continued walking. "Dan, I don't want to get too personal, but it's a mystery to us all why you stay at St. Martin's? You kind of gave me a sense just now, but we're all still baffled."

Dan lit up a smoke, exhaled, and said, "I don't know. Maybe it's the structure I like, maybe I'm in a groove, maybe it's the Catholic thing."

'Ehhhh, I know a thing or two about that — not a lot of commitment there anymore. People aren't sticking with it."

Dan stopped and looked at Joe, "I know, Joe. I know that."

· · · · ·

"It's time to break out the secret weapon," Vito said as he climbed out of his cart at the sixteenth green. "Joey and I have got to put some distance between us and you two birds. This game is a little too close for comfort. He reached in his bag and pulled out a putter that had a head that looked like a glass paperweight.

"What did you do, open a new account at the bank?" Roger shouted from the water fountain.

"Hey, no smart-ass comments. This little club is a gift from my brother Tony. It's got a built-in radar system, can't fail."

"Is it sanctioned by the PGA?"

"I'll sanction you, Roge!"

"You're away," said Dan, removing the pin.

"Come on you little honey, do it for me, for our team," said Vito. He stood over the ball, gently slid his putter back, and came forward striking the ball, a little too hard. It rolled toward the cup with too much speed, caught the lip of the cup and kept going another ten feet. "Shit!"

"So much for the secret weapon," Roger said.

"Listen, numb nuts, I am just warming this baby up."

"Sure, and two holes to go," Roger said and then watched his putt come within an inch of the cup. "I'll tap this one in." Picking his ball out the cup, he said, "Sink yours, Dan, and we have these guys on the ropes."

Dan had been studying his shot. Now he stood over the ball and struck it smoothly. It rolled to the edge of the cup and dropped in. "I'll take a five."

"Good God, these guys are putting heat on us, Vito," Joe said and then looked down at the ball. He made his stroke — the ball approached, seemed to die, and then picked up a touch of speed and fell in. "Ah, that feels soooo good."

Vito's putt with the secret weapon fell about a foot short and he tapped in. "Did either of you guys pay off my brother to give me this piece of crap?"

· · · · ·

On the eighteenth hole, Roger sliced his ball into the woods, and since there was no group behind them, he took a few moments to search for the ball while Dan sat in the cart smoking a cigarette. Roger moved some brush with one of his irons. "Oh, Dan, I forgot to mention that Missy and I saw Kate last Friday on the Dutch Apple cruise. We said hello — she was with some Attorney from the education department — Bob somebody." Roger stooped to look at a ball. "What happened, Dan, between you two? You seemed to have it going pretty well."

Dan butted his cigarette out on the ground, "Let me help you look."

"Another minute, and I'll throw a new ball out. Hey, listen, if I'm prying too much, just tell me."

"Top Flight?" Dan said, holding up a ball.

"Taylor," Roger said, "hang on to that one."

"Sure, I'll let you know if you are. Let's just say that it was a matter of life style. Maybe I was a little too slow for Kate."

"And one of the things was that you were still at St. Martin's?"

"Yes," said Dan picking up a somewhat battered ball and heaving it into the woods. "That and a few other things."

"Like the fact that a person with your smarts wasn't moving in the right direction?"

"I guess, sort of the stuck in a rut idea. Here's your ball."

"Thanks, flip it out on the fairway for me, and let's catch up to the senior citizens."

· · · · ·

172

As they approached the 150 yard marker, it seemed to Dan that everyone except their foursome had left the golf course. The tall pines behind the eighteenth green created a silent backdrop to the stage where two figures, one in red and one in yellow, were slowly approaching tiny specs of white. It was so still. Dan had ceased the discussion with Roger, who, like the rest, had boarded the express out of St. Martin's. And he had stayed. In a way, that decision made it easy to offer an explanation about his breakup with Kate. It was language commonly understood. "Okay, I'll get off here, Roger, and walk in."

Roger eased the cart to a stop, "Good, I'll swing the cart behind the green and grab your putter."

"Thanks, Roger," Dan said reaching for his seven iron, a gift from Father Charles. After Father Charles had given Dan his old set of clubs, he handed him one more club. "Dan," Father Charles had said, "I am going to give you a special club, a gift to me years ago from a close friend. I want you to have it — my game of golf is almost done, but I want you to have this club. It's got Ben Hogan's signature on it, and I always felt that "the Hogan" served me well, especially at crucial times. I used it pretty regularly from about 150, but I also used it to chip with it at times. Great iron."

Approaching the ball, Dan paused and looked down at the green where the red and yellow shirts lined up with the blue flag to form a triangle. He took his practice swings — three times — and then stepped to the ball. He got into a comfortable position, breathed in once and exhaled, and then swung the club. It may have been his best swing of the day. The ball rose above the green and then began its descent falling slowly as if in a dream onto the green, maybe eight feet from the pin. Now he saw Vito and Joe raise their clubs in praise. And Vito's shouted words, "What the hell,

Dan? Saving the best for last?" And Dan could see Father Charles with a huge smile.

· · · · ·

Two months earlier, in the rectory at St. Leo's, Dan had put Father Charles' optimism to the test. "I am deadly serious, Father, I never felt like hitting anyone before, as an adult that is, until Doyle showed up. Jesus, Father, I wish you were still around the school."

"Dan," Father Charles said, leaning back in his chair and exhaling a puff of cigar smoke, "I'm retired for good. I have a few chores around the parish, and thank the Lord, Father Russell has given me a daily Mass. I can't go over to the high school and start inserting my opinions, not the way I used to. But tell me, what's going on with Father Doyle?"

"Well, I don't think I can count all the little things, some of them seem petty, like not saying hello in the hallway or rarely saying thank you — let me rephrase that — never saying thank you for anything." Dan paused to light a cigarette. "I know you said that he is one of these perfectionists, and I've been willing to give him some time, and the guy does have some ideas that seem to have weight, but he's parsimonious with sharing much of anything — or he presents his idea in a pronouncement — as a finished product."

"I see," said Father Charles who had stood up. "A little touch more of tea?"

"Yes, it's excellent."

"Black Raspberry, my sister brought it back from The Mount, Edith Wharton's home in Lenox."

Father Charles poured for both of them, "Go on with your story."

"Well, I know I told you things had gotten pretty bad, so let me get to the proverbial straw that is threatening to break this camel's back." Dan sat up in his chair. "Last Wednesday I find this note in my mailbox to see Doyle after school. So I stop in, and he gets up and closes the door. Then he makes this proposal to me, but not really a proposal, that he take my Honors English class next year, and if I didn't mind would I take a new section of non-Regents juniors instead, kids with a lot of needs. I think I sat there speechless and just stared. He then tells me that he was a classics major in college and did some teaching in the seminary for a few years. And he says, 'I would really like to get back into a little teaching, and to be honest, I feel very comfortable with Homer, Virgil, Sophocles, Euripides... and the rest of them.'"

Father Charles brushed a few strands of grey hair off his forehead, "Did you say anything?"

"I said I would like to think about it. And then he quickly added that having the slow juniors would actually give me more time to work on curriculum development. I knew my face was getting flushed in front of him. Part of me couldn't believe what I was hearing. Then I found myself suddenly standing and saying that I had to see some student about the literary magazine, and I walked out."

"Dan, I think you have to be very forthright and up front with him — I know how much that course means to you. If you don't want him to take the course that you designed and that you teach very well, you just have to say that."

"Too late, Father. Friday, I got my schedule for next fall, and guess what I am not teaching."

Father Charles placed his teacup on the small table next to his chair. "He never got back to you before doing that?"

"Nope, and in Friday's faculty bulletin, he let the whole faculty know that in order to better appreciate the hard work of the staff and to connect a little better with the students he has decided to teach one course next year and, after consulting with Dan Richardson, he has selected Honors English. Father, I don't think I can take this crap, especially the way the bastard did it."

"Dan, you can't let one horse's ass drive you out of St. Martin's. We need people like you. God knows, you have done a great job at that school. I don't want to see St. Martin's lose you. Listen, there may be a way. We have a deanery meeting in a couple of weeks, and Doyle always attends. Let me see if I can isolate the guy and do a little educating of my own. We need you, Dan."

Father Charles leaned forward and extended his right hand. Dan put out his right hand and met Father Charles' hand. Then Father Charles covered the two hands with his left. "Don't do anything drastic for a while, Dan, and it might even mean holding out for a year. Time can sometimes be your best friend. And, Dan, you know that I will be here whenever you need me."

. . . . .

Three weeks after he had received a contract for the next school year, Dan received a note in his mailbox. "Dan, I had a long talk with Father Charles after the deanery meeting. He went on for some time extolling you as one of the finest teachers at St. Martin's. He also pointed out, as I well know, that you put a great deal of time and energy into Honors English with extensive bibliographies, reading lists, and very creative assignments. That information was very helpful. When you have the time over the next week or two, please xerox for me any additional material that you think would facilitate my teaching of the Honors

English class. I am so eager to step back into the class-room." Father Doyle

. . . . .

Approaching the apron of the eighteenth, Dan thought of the anger he had felt after reading Doyle's note. Now with over two months gone by, he felt good about the fact that he had not acceded to Doyle's request to turn over his best material. He still burned inside, and he wasn't sure how he would make it through the year, but maybe he could turn that anger into something else.

"Dan, my man," Roger had pulled the pin and placed it several feet away from the cup, "I think your seven iron is our secret weapon. That may have sealed it."

"Hey, Roge, don't jump the gun yet." Vito said pointing his putter at Roger. "We still have to finish. Joe is away."

Dan couldn't help but smile at Vito - he was so pre-dictable. He watched Joe's putt move up the slight incline and stop about five feet short of the cup. "Shit," Vito said. "What the hell? Roger, you're up."

Roger moved forward, took a practice putt, and then stepped into position, and struck the ball firmly. Rolling right to the cup, it appeared to be a sure thing, but then stopped right at the lip and hung there.

"Quiet everyone," Vito said, "we don't want to disturb the ball."

Roger stood over the ball watching and hoping, and then tapped it in.

"Well, Dan-boy," Vito said, "I guess I'm next. I'm not saying that we need this putt to win, but seeing this baby go in to close out the day will be pretty sweet." The ball he struck was off line and ended up three feet to the right of the pin.

"Son of a bitch. Let me finish up and I'll give you the green." Vito's ball hit the back of the cup and dropped in.

"I'm not getting too excited, but I can taste those two rounds of beer," Roger said.

Once again, everything seemed so still to Dan. He felt as if he was on a stage, and everyone was waiting for his word. The cup was maybe ten feet away, and the green sloped slightly to the left. Hit it a little on the high side he thought. He could see the line form in front of him, so clearly. His breathing was even. He took the putter back smoothly, came forward with just the right flow meeting the ball evenly, and it rode the line he had created right into the cup.

"My man," Roger shouted.

"You did it, Dan," said Joe, pulling his shirt away from his body. "What an end!"

"I'll give you that," said Vito, "I'll give you that freaking putt."

Dan walked to the cup, reached down, and picked up his ball. He stood looking at the ball for a second and then uttered a loud sigh. He turned to Vito, smiled, and lifted his hand for a high five, "Thanks, Vito," and then gave the same closing to Roger and Joe.

Back to the Light

On the way down the staircase from the faculty room after a frustrating and futile engagement with the Xerox machine, I pass the Christmas Manger outside the chapel and head toward my classroom. The hall is dark except for the Manger light, which is now behind me. I fumble through my keys until I feel the smooth key that opens my classroom door. I touch the light switch just inside the door and enter my room. It is Sunday night about 7 p.m.

On my desk is a reminder that Friday had been the last day to bring in unwrapped toys for children who will come to the City Mission and have the chance to select a gift they like. Those students in my homeroom who forgot to bring in a gift were relieved to hear on the Friday afternoon announcements that the time had been extended until Tuesday.

From my file cabinet, I select a few exercises for Monday's classes, place them neatly on my desk, and then take a seat in a rocking chair that was my mother's. She who had longed to become a teacher would be thrilled at the placement of her rocker in the front of the classroom. From this chair, books from every genre are within easy reach. I rock slowly remembering my mother's little alternating movement of her feet when she rocked, almost as if she were walking, and then look up to see my reflection in the classroom windows. Past my reflection, I see snow drifting down in front of headlights as the cars pass on by. I wonder if the drivers are wondering who that person is in the only lit classroom in the building.

To my right, I see my now open door decorated with a "Christmas in Ireland" theme. Each homeroom had chosen a theme for their door, and when one walked down the hallway, you could see the rich variety of seasonal themes from different countries.

To my left on the bookcase built by my father is a small artificial Christmas tree my wife bought me years ago. It has held up well. On the wall above the speakers of my turntable is a smiling Bob Dylan and to his right a poster of Miles Davis holding a trumpet and looking pensive. I pause and reflect on the two expressions. Maybe a smile and a pensive look speak to the heart of the season.

In John Cheever's story "Christmas Is a Sad Season for the Poor," Charlie, the central character, thinks about the poor children in his neighborhood. "Every time they took a walk, they'd see all the expensive toys in the store windows, and they'd write letters to Santa Claus, and their fathers and mothers would promise to mail them, and after the kids had gone to sleep, they'd burn the letters in the stove."

To his amazement on Christmas day, Charlie, who operates an elevator in an apartment complex, is deluged with gifts and offers of dinner from the many tenants he has served. In a moment of joy, he celebrates by using the elevator as an amusement park ride and is fired. Momentarily stunned, he then looks around at all he has been given and thinks of his own landlady and her three skinny children.

After Charlie has delivered all his presents to his landlady, she watches her own children, surrounded by presents, some opened, many still to be opened, and she says, "You kids have got your share. Now a nice thing to do would be to take all this stuff that's left over to those poor people on Hudson Street — the Deckers. They ain't got nothing."

Nothing. In the landlady's words is the heart of the season: to give to those who have nothing; to be a light in the dark, snow-filled night. I have seen it in the classroom. A student, quiet and intelligent, writes an essay about how he and his mom, without much more than the basic means to get by, approach each day with thought and care and love. Another student, asked to define a hero, writes, "A hero is not just someone who wins a battle, but someone who will go to an extreme to change someone else's life for the better." And another student slips two dollars onto a desk to someone who has no lunch.

I gaze about the room — the desks are shining, the walls a montage of photographs, calendars, quotations, the bookcases overflowing with books. The room is empty of students, but it's not nothing. It is comfortable in here. Once again, Hemingway's clean, well-lighted place comes to mind. I rock a bit more, and then it's time to go. I get up from the rocker and head for the door, the words Nollaig Shona over the door's window. My hand touches the light switch, and I step out into the near darkness. The only light visible is the one over the Manger.

PAUL O'BRIEN taught English at Notre Dame and Notre Dame-Bishop Gibbons for forty-seven years. Since leaving the classroom, he has remained active on the Notre Dame-Bishop Gibbons School Board, the St. Kateri Tekakwitha School Board, the New York State English Council Executive Board, and UCALL —Union College Adult Lifetime Learning. His hobbies include reading, writing, traveling, and dining out. He lives in Niskayuna, New York, with his wife Deborah and cat Casey.